CN01467252

THE CODEPENDENCY RECOVERY BLUEPRINT

FROM PEOPLE-PLEASING, LOW SELF-ESTEEM &
INTIMACY ISSUES OF A CODEPENDENT TO
EMOTIONAL INTELLIGENCE, SELF-CONFIDENCE &
SELF-CARING OF AN INDEPENDENT

DON BARLOW

A ROADTOTRANQUILITY BOOK

CONTENTS

© **Copyright 2019 - All rights reserved.**

The content contained within this book may not be reproduced, duplicated or transmitted without direct written permission from the author or the publisher.

Under no circumstances will any blame or legal responsibility be held against the publisher, or author, for any damages, reparation, or monetary loss due to the information contained within this book, either directly or indirectly.

Legal Notice:

This book is copyright protected. It is only for personal use. You cannot amend, distribute, sell, use, quote or paraphrase any part, or the content within this book, without the consent of the author or publisher.

Disclaimer Notice:

Please note the information contained within this document is for educational and entertainment purposes only. All effort has been executed to present accurate, up to date, reliable, complete information. No warranties of any kind are declared or implied. Readers acknowledge that the publisher and author are not engaged in the rendering of legal, financial, medical or professional advice. The content within this book has been derived from various sources. Please consult a licensed professional before attempting any techniques outlined in this book.

By reading this document, the reader agrees that under no circumstances is the publisher, or author, responsible for any losses, direct or indirect, that are incurred as a result of the use of the information contained within this document, including, but not limited to, errors, omissions, or inaccuracies.

Names in this book have been changed to protect the privacy of those individuals.

PEOPLE PLEASING

NO MORE

START SAYING NO

LEARN TO SAY NO WITHOUT
EXPLAINING YOURSELF

DON BARLOW

Before we get into the book, let me offer you a free mini-book. Scan this QR code to claim your FREE People-Pleasing No More mini-book!

INTRODUCTION

"Daring to set boundaries is about having the courage to love ourselves even when we risk disappointing others."

— BRENE BROWN

Have you lost sight of who you are as an individual? If you find yourself questioning the healthiness of your relationships and struggle to stand up for what you want, you're not alone. Codependent behaviors are some of the most difficult relationship patterns to identify, yet it's rarely discussed and often considered another form of "clinginess". This definition ignores the feelings of guilt and shame that arise from the best of intentions—it does nothing to recognize that even the best intentions can hurt. As you put yourself on the line for the people you love, it can be difficult to tell when the boundaries between you and them have blurred to the point of toxicity. After all, you're motivated by wanting the best for others, even if it means you have to put aside your own values and opinions to do so. However, when you come to rely on outside factors for validation and a sense of identity, these "do good" habits can do more harm than good. You may suddenly feel obligated to stay in a constricting relationship that turns you into a victim and limits your capacity for intimacy. It can feel as though you have no one to turn to because everybody relies on you. That doesn't mean your life has to stay that way. Codependency may be running your life, but you are the one in the driver's seat. In fact, you've already taken the first step by realizing you need to change the path you're on. I know firsthand the transformational effects of recovering from codependency and have compiled the knowledge I've gained over the years so others can experience the same freedom.

Can you imagine basing your day on which side of the bed your spouse, boss, parent, boyfriend or girlfriend gets up on? Codependency is characterized by an individual participating in a relationship that is one-sided; that has a complete lack of mutual respect; and in which one of the individuals nearly relies completely on the other to meet 100 percent of their emotional needs. Codependent individuals live with their confidence and self-esteem depending on another person. Codependency has often been synonymous with the term 'enabler', in which helping through enabling allows another individual to maintain unhealthy behaviors, including not working and other irresponsible actions, drug and alcohol abuse, gambling addiction, shopping addiction, sex addictions (addictions, in general), and abusive tendencies toward the codependent person who is enabling them. Codependency is exhausting because it requires a great deal of energy to meet another person's needs. Here's the good news. Codependency can be treated. It is a behavior that is learned and usually passed down through generations. Sometimes referred to as a "relationship addiction", it affects one's chances of having healthy and happy relationships that are based on mutual respect.

The term codependency has evolved a great deal since its beginning back in 1936. The founders of Alcoholics Anonymous (AA), Bill W. and Dr. Bob started the most successful treatment for alcoholism known today. Shortly afterward, Lois W. (Bill W.'s wife) and Anne B. (Dr. Bob's wife) started another twelve-step group meeting for the family members of alcoholics to attend. Of course, it seems only natural that living with an addict would bring a multitude of problems into any family. By the 1970s, addiction professionals started realizing that treating the addict only was insufficient; the whole family, and possibly close friends needed treatment, as well.

The term codependency has been greatly widened to include many aspects and behavioral traits of individuals living in a dysfunctional family atmosphere. Dysfunctional families often lack boundaries, or the boundaries are so blurred that each member takes on the problems of the others, creating a snowball effect of troubles. Dysfunctional family members suffer from anger issues, shame, fear, and feelings of isolation because their emotions have been ignored and love is often conditional. There are usually underlying issues, such as addiction to food, drugs, alcohol, sex, gambling, or problematic relationships. Other underlying issues include family members suffering from mental or physical illness, various types of abuse, a lack of communication, and repressed fear. They have developed ways of dissociating from difficult emotions and have learned how to not confront any problems. This can lead to serious trust issues and even physical illness. Most dysfunctional families attribute their main focus to the 'identified patient'—the addict or sick one—and then a codependency will develop, and the individual will sacrifice their own needs to devote their time to fixing the sick person. With time, loss of identity sets in and reality becomes distorted.

Codependent individuals seek stimulation from the outside to help them feel better. Some may delve into their jobs and become compulsive workaholics. While they have the best intentions trying to tend to the person having the difficulties, their efforts are often self-defeating. Taking on a martyr's role and becoming the beneficiary of another's needs can become compulsive in nature. We have all heard the phrase 'pulling some strings' to keep someone from having consequences. The issue here is that the problems repeat themselves in a never-ending cycle. The codependent behavior is reinforced by the individual feeling rewarded because they feel needed. As the cycle continues on a destructive course, the codependent increasingly becomes less healthy until they feel no choice but to keep doing it. The codependent person views themselves as a victim; one who is attracted to people in need. It isn't selfish to put yourself first—it's time to prioritize your own life and happiness and stop ignoring your personal needs. Listen to your instincts, and take this first step on your journey to finding independence and fulfilment.

In this book, you will find what you need to learn:

- What codependency is and isn't, as well as its historical background.
- Exercises and practices to help break the pattern of enabling others while learning to assert yourself.
- How childhood experiences contribute to dysfunctional relationships and determine the behaviors that follow you into adulthood.
- The five patterns of codependent behavior, and how identifying them will help you understand the signs and symptoms manifesting in your life.
- Techniques and advice for getting over your need for control and learning to accept people for who they are.
- Identifying the three stages of codependency progression; how to begin the recovery process by reclaiming your sense of identity and self-worth.
- Essential self-care practices that promote self-respect and compassion, even in difficult situations.
- How habits form.
- The Twelve-Step Recovery Program.

1

CODEPENDENCY, NOT CLINGINESS

The healthy characteristics of depending upon one another have been present throughout history; humans have always relied on social support from important relationships. As noted in the introduction to the book, the definition of codependency is a long way from its original meaning in 1936 and 1970s. The significant others of those afflicted revealing dysfunctional behaviors were called *co-chemically dependent*. Shortly afterward, the term was shortened to *codependent*. When the 1980s rolled around, addiction (including alcoholism) was referred to as *chemical dependency*. During this period, the disease model spearheaded the concept of codependency. One reason for labeling codependency a disease is because of its progressive nature. As the individual(s) around the codependent become sicker, the codependent behaviors become intensified. What may have started as overly concerned can snowball into depression, isolation, mental and physical illness in the codependent, and sometimes even suicidal ideations. Another element to the disease model of codependency is that the self-destructive behaviors associated with the condition become habitual, just like the drink or the drug for the addict.

In the 1980s, the codependent personality model was coined and dealt with the condition in terms of diagnosis, treatment, and clinical interventions. This model focused on the predisposed factors in the development of the personality of the codependent. The interactionist model of codependency puts forth a duo of intrapersonal and interpersonal elements necessary in the development and necessary to maintain their dysfunctional lifestyle. During the 1980s codependency, as a condition, was used to delineate people who were in any type of significant relationship with an addict, narcissist, borderline personality and other personality disorders. Codependency definition is aimed toward those whose life seemed unbearable unless focused on their partner; they struggled with individualization. At first, the characteristics seemed to be weak, overly emotional, needed and clingy. In present times, codependency is a common term used by professionals and laypeople, alike. There is some discussion about changing the term to 'self-love deficit disorder', because at the very center of codependency, a lack of self-love is evident. In summation, codependency is a pathological interactional condition developed by the codependent, honing into self-injurious actions that are connected to the psychogenetics of the codependent's dysfunctional family environment whilst growing up.

What determines the severity of codependency in a person?

- Genetics;
- Culture and religious beliefs;
- Family dynamics;
- Dysfunctional families are often predictors of codependent behavior;
- Childhood abuse and chronic physical abuse also promote codependency;
- Past trauma experiences;
- Role models;
- Codependency is a learned behavior, so if you had role models growing up (such as your parents or older siblings) who displayed codependent tendencies, you are more likely to develop them, as well;
- Use of substances, such as drugs and alcohol;
- Many codependent relationships develop when one partner feels they need to step up and support a struggling addict;
- Drugs and alcohol can also make it more difficult for the involved parties to recognize that something is wrong; and
- The relationships a person has had with addicts and other co-dependent people.

Who does codependency affect?

It affects more than just the struggling addict; codependency affects all of the immediate and extended family members, colleagues, friends and anyone else involved in the addict's life. The sad truth of the matter is that one common problem among addicts is the involvement of their loved ones in helping them to protect and conceal their addiction and even accepting it. The members of a dysfunctional family might, without intention, play a part in the addiction of their loved one, therefore, the codependency affects the addict. Often the codependent doesn't reveal that they know there is a problem with their loved one and may ignore or deny the problem even when it is staring them right in the face. The codependent family does not need to take responsibility for the problems their loved one is facing, and they have to keep in mind their own needs. The individual must say out loud that they did not create the problems of the afflicted one and therefore, are not responsible for fixing them. While the codependent has the best intentions in mind when trying to help a loved one, all they really do is perpetuate the afflicted one's illness by trying to protect them. Sometimes refusing to bail them out leads to a much healthier outcome. The longer the codependent rescues the afflicted individual either physically, financially or criminally, the longer the afflicted doesn't learn from their mistakes and continue with the dysfunctional actions. It is sometimes surprising to the codependent that they were enabling their loved one to continue with their addiction or abusive behavior patterns, which was allowing them to continue down the path of destruction. Having a codependent relationship can develop into a dangerous state of being, especially if an addiction is involved. The enabling behaviors cycle and the addiction will continue until a crisis or intervention happens to break the cycle. Unfortunately, and often tragic situations, such as a car crash, loss of employment, divorce, bankruptcy, overdose, and even death of the individual of whom is enabled are the consequences of codependency.

Despite people's best intentions, many often find themselves replicating the same unhealthy patterns in their relationships. If two individuals with maladjusted personality types come together, their dysfunctional traits worsen. *Enmeshment* is a term describing the relationship between family members or couples in which the boundaries are so unclear that the people involved take on the emotions of another to the extent that they experience the anger, sadness, happiness, rage, etc. when the other does. In a dysfunctional family, when codependency is present, the entire group can act as one in ways that are unhealthy for everyone involved. Think about couples you have met (hopefully you are not part of this duo; but if so, there is help.) in which their relationship is so toxic you wonder how on earth they are staying together. Outsiders need to realize that both people in the problematic relationship are there by choice. Some say they are staying together for various important reasons, such as the children, money, fear of divorce shaming, and how much time they have invested. The actual bigger picture is a belief that one or both in the couple think they deserve to be treated poorly.

When born into this world, we are completely dependent on our parents for safety, warmth and food. The bond between an infant and its caregivers is imperative for survival, both emotionally and physically. Hence, dependency on others starts at birth. If, when growing up, the caregiver is inconsistent or unavailable, the child takes on the role of caretaker. This results in the child putting the needs of their parents first. In a dysfunctional family, there is no acknowledgement of feelings or that there even is a problem resulting in the family members holding in their emotions and disregarding their own needs so they can focus on the needs of their parents. When this same child who has been *parentified* becomes an adult, they fall into the same pattern with their relationships.

When an individual doesn't recognize their own wants and needs because they are focused on another person's needs, resentment builds, and the tendency for overreactions or lashing out in anger happens when their partner lets them down in some way. The codependent partner feels a lack of internal control, so they seek validation from the outside by trying to control their significant other's behaviors. When finding out this control cannot be maintained, the codependent becomes disappointed and can slide into depression. While it is completely normal to feel partially responsible for those you love, it is unhealthy when your identity is contingent upon another. Even if you do not feel this way at the start, and even enjoy feeling needed and relied upon, it can be carried to an extremely unhealthy degree as the relationship progresses. Once the relationship has become unhealthy, it can become hard to get out of the dysfunctional relationship, since you feel so relied upon—even when you know leaving is the right thing to do.

It is obvious that relationships can be tricky, and for the codependent, it is difficult to find the right balance between being close to someone and having personal space. If you find yourself leaning toward the clingy direction, here are some helpful suggestions for reeling in your clingy ways and giving your partner some space:

1. Identify the trust issues you need to work on. While it seems that everyone knows how important it is to trust your significant others; if you don't, it becomes impossible to give

them the necessary space for them to live as an individual capable of sharing a healthy relationship with you. A lack of trust usually breeds resentment in your partner. The root of the matter is: "Why is there a lack of trust?" Constantly checking their cell phone messages, Facebook newsfeed, and emails can lead to a horrible existence for both involved.

2. Let your partner have their space. Too much togetherness can put a strain on your relationship and can often lead to feelings of entrapment and suffocation. By giving your partner space, they are less likely to have a negative paired association.

3. Focus on centering yourself. You will be amazed at how much you can learn about yourself when you are alone. Showing your partner that you are not dependent on them for your every thought and need is more attractive.

4. Clinginess happens when the codependent life becomes centered solely around their partner. It is imperative that you have your own interests and goals as a priority. Rather than obsessively focusing on your partner, turn your attention inward toward something constructive.

5. Avoid making your partner responsible for your nervousness or anxiety. Simply employ some healthy stress management techniques to quell your fears and relax your body.

6. Watch your body language, such as an excessive need to communicate affection. Clinginess can be emotional and psychological as much as it is physical. Respect other people's boundaries. Some individuals do not like to be touched too much.

SYMPTOMS OF CODEPENDENCY

Poor boundaries: Boundaries are what divides what is yours and what belongs to someone else. Poor boundary setting is when there is a blurred line between where you begin and someone else ends. Codependent individuals usually struggle with setting clear boundaries. Boundary setting applies to not only your belongings, but your body, needs, money, and your thoughts. Codependent individuals feel responsible for how the people in their lives are feeling and often blame their own feelings or problems on those people. Healthy boundaries indicate what you will and what you won't be responsible for. In the workplace, or in relationships that are very personal, having poor boundaries can lead to feelings of resentment, exhaustion and sometimes anger. In general, having poor boundaries can lead to financial troubles, poor time management, relationship problems, and stress, all of which can cause mental anguish.

Low self-esteem: Self-esteem is a reflection of how you think and feel about yourself. It is essentially a self-appraisal. It is your true opinion of who you are. A low self-esteem is an emotion of feeling that you're not good enough, especially when comparing yourself to others. Sometimes self-esteem is portrayed in a disguise when the person actually feels unlovable. Feelings of shame and guilt and trying to be a perfectionist go hand-in-hand with low self-esteem. Instead of a healthy degree of self-evaluation, the codependent turns to other people for validation and to access their own value. It is other individuals who can make the codependent feel badly or good about themselves; which is why codependent is also described as *other-defined*. Due to feeling disconnected from their inner self, codependents struggle with self-trust and become confused when trying to develop their own opinions. They are unsure of what they really want and have to defer to others to feel liked or loved. Often when they know their own desires and needs, they talk themselves out of them or dismiss them to go along with someone else to avoid any conflict, especially in a tight-knit relationship. The table below compares the signs of high self-esteem and low self-esteem:

High Self-Esteem	Low Self-Esteem
I am fine the way I am.	I am not enough. I have to improve.
I accept praise.	I doubt or deflect praise.
I am efficient.	I lack confidence.
I have self-respect.	I lack compassion and respect for myself.
I am a compassionate person.	I am overly sensitive and judgmental of others.
I trust my decisions.	I am never sure if I am making the right decision.
I am a competent person.	I rely on others to tell me if I am doing OK.
I am honest.	I will say whatever I need to say to gain approval or please someone else.
I know I am of value.	I have low self-worth.
I want to be helpful.	I have to be needed.
I am only responsible for my actions.	I am responsible for the needs and actions of those I care about.

High self-esteem does not change due to external events. People with good self-esteem do not feel badly about themselves when bad things occur because those events are external and, therefore, not a reflection of one's inner being. But, when a person's self-esteem is low and bad things happen, they suffer disappointment or loss and feel defeated. It is important to remember that, when your self-esteem is low, you can become critical of yourself to the extreme, finding fault with all that you do, wear, say or create. Self-loathing can set in, giving rise to feelings of humiliation and embarrassment.

Controlling another person because of insufficient boundary setting and thinking of it as being in a caretaking role is another example of codependency. Feeling the imperative need to tell others what they should or should not do in order to get them to behave the way you want them to. Codependents often need to feel control over others in order to feel OK, themselves. Therefore, they tend to violate other people's boundaries. Codependents have often been through situations in life with individuals who were out of control, leaving the codependent feeling disappointed and sorrowful. They become fearful of allowing other people to let their life events happen naturally and to be who they are. The codependent doesn't acknowledge their loss of control anxiety and thinks they know what is best for someone else. They try their darndest to control other people with manipulations of helplessness, domination, guilt, advice, coercion, etc. and finally end up failing in their efforts to change the person or provoke the desired reaction. The only time a codependent feels safe is when the power is tilted toward them and the significant other has insecurities. When a partner is insecure, the codependent can get to work on "fixing" them. In this instance, the codependent feels they are in control, so they agree and comply with their partner while doing everything possible to give the impression that all is well. They generally do not want a significant other to feel secure so they can keep their fears of rejection and abandonment at bay. They will use non-subtle and very subtle techniques, such as passive-aggression (i.e., the silent treatment) and playing the victim to undermine their partner's feelings of security. Also, they are on high alert for any changes in their partner's behavior or mood that may indicate a turn in the tide in either direction.

Poor communication skills plague the codependent person. When it comes to talking about their own emotions, thoughts, and needs, the codependent individual is afraid to communicate their true feelings in fear of upsetting someone else. It leads the codependent toward manipulation and dishonesty. Codependents struggle with anxiety when it comes to being truthful; they do not want to disappoint anyone. So, rather than saying, "That is not OK," they may pretend that it is OK or give advice on how to be more OK. The communication becomes less than honest and confusing to others. Good communication requires an ability to be assertive and to include the person with whom you are trying to talk to by listening to what they say and showing empathy toward their feelings.

With healthy communication, there is no threatening feelings or the need to agree all of the time. Sometimes compromise is necessary, but there is comfort in expressing your thoughts and opinions, as well as taking the responsibility for what you have said. People's communication styles are developed in childhood. With encouragement, a child learns how to express their feelings, and likes and dislikes in the right manner. This carries on into adulthood. If the child was shamed and came from a dysfunctional family, they develop survival tactics that are unhealthy. Learning to lie and manipulate others to get their needs met becomes a common coping strategy, as well as people pleasing and the inability to handle anger. Relationships become damaged when the patterns of communication are unhealthy. The codependent relationship can become distant, abusive, and controlling without good communication. In turn, this leads to low self-esteem and stops the growth of healthy emotions.

Fear is the underlying force behind the way a codependent communicates. By masquerading as the truth, fear keeps the codependent feeling a false sense of unworthiness and that other people's reactions can destroy their very being. Therefore, fear is often reflected in the communication patterns of the codependent (i.e., walking on eggshells). But, in some instances, when dealing with an angry person, a codependent has made a real habit out of being dishonest and unresponsive, as to avoid any confrontation. If closely examined, the attitudes and feelings behind the way codependents communicate are grounded in shame, lack of commitment, lack of self-worth, anger and fear of abandonment—all based on dishonest communication within themselves. Every time they fail to pay tribute to their own precious feelings and thoughts for the sake of pleasing others, the codependent sells themselves short. Their true self might be periled in agony while the codependent walks around with a smile on their face.

Abandonment: Codependents are dependent on other people's feelings about them. Often, the codependent person has abandonment issues, fear rejection, and obsessively worry about saying or doing the wrong thing (according to someone else's standards). Because of their abandonment fears, they often will stay in an unhealthy relationship, leading them to feel trapped and depressed.

Codependents tend to encounter abandonment in relationships that mirrors the feelings of abandonment they experienced as a child from either one or both of their parents. All children need to feel accepted and loved by both of their parents in order to develop good self-esteem and good self-worth. A parent can't just say "I love you" to their child; they need to do/say more, especially because they are responsible for the healthy development of their child. They need to express their love through actions and words showing they desire a close relationship with their child while respecting the child's individuality. This includes having empathy for the child's needs and feelings. When the parent of a child criticizes, dismisses, or is preoccupied with themselves, they are not capable of empathizing with their child's needs or emotions. In turn, the child is left feeling misunderstood, hurt, emotionally abandoned, ashamed, and alone. Even when giving a child much attention, if the parent is not attuned to their needs, which, therefore, go unmet, it is still *emotional abandonment*. Feelings of abandonment arise when a child experiences feeling unimportant. As the cycle continues, the child, now an adult, fears intimacy. They tend to shy away from partners who want close intimacy because the distance is familiar and makes them feel safe. If the relationship starts moving in the direction of more intimacy, the distance will be recreated through arguments, infidelity, abuse, or addiction, further confirming the codependent's feelings of hopelessness, and self-perceptions of being unlovable. If these components put an end to the relationship, it fuels the fear of abandonment even more, leading to more hopelessness and the codependent's inability to verbalize their feelings.

Caretaking to an unhealthy extreme is a prime example of poor boundaries. Caregiving is not the same as codependent care-taking. It is normal to feel sympathy and empathy for another, but to put their needs ahead of yours is not normal. The codependent is set on fixing someone else, rescuing them, and controlling them even when the person ignores their attempt. Such is the case where addictions are involved. There are critical differences between caregiving and care-taking; the more caregiving and not caretaking the happier and healthier you are. Caretaking is a learned dysfunctional codependent behavior that can absolutely be unlearned. The main goal here is for the codependent to learn to decrease their caretaking while providing caregiving, leading to a more peaceful and more content quality of life. Truthfully, caretaking is the central element of codependency, as it is based on the need for control and is deeply rooted in insecurity. On the other hand, caregiving is based on love and compassion. All relationships involve a degree of give and take. Caregiving doesn't feel like a compulsion or obligation, and instead is the natural flow of support in a dynamic relationship. Codependent caregiving is unbalanced and perpetuates a cycle of imbalance in the relationship. The following are some of the main differences between caregiving and caretaking:

1. Caregiving is inspirational, energizing and feels like love. Caretaking is exhausting, stressful and frustrating.
2. Caregivers honor boundaries, while caretakers blur the boundaries.
3. Caregivers give of themselves freely while caretakers do just that. They take from the person they are helping because there are conditions for the care.
4. Caregivers take care of themselves because they understand that "a happy, healthy me" enables them to be of assistance to others. Caretakers do not take good care of themselves

in fear of being viewed as selfish and having low self-worth.

5. Caregivers actively take measures for solving problems. Caretakers incessantly worry and become preoccupied with thoughts and not actions.

6. Caregivers have a good sense of who they are and know what is best for themselves. Caretakers believe they know what is best for someone else.

7. Caregivers trust other people to help with problem-solving, based on their own capabilities. Caretakers think they are the only ones with the right answers and do not trust others in the care for themselves.

8. The act of giving care lowers anxiety levels and gives the caregiver a rewarding feeling regarding participating in helping another individual. The act of taking care of others creates great angst and/or a depressive state.

9. Caregivers engage more with healthy people either at their own or slightly above their own degree of mental health. Caretakers engage in relationships with needy people.

10. Caregivers are non-judgmental, and caretakers tend to be very judgmental while giving a false appearance of non-judgmentalism.

11. Caregivers show empathy and wait for the one in need to let them know when they need help from them. Caretakers jump into rescue mode as soon as *they* notice a problem in someone else's life.

12. Caregivers are solution driven, while caretakers are attention-seeking in their dramatic actions with the problem.

13. Caregivers refer to "you" a lot. Caretakers refer to "I" much more than "you".

Denial and more denial are prevalent in the codependent personality. Blaming others and never owning the problem allows the codependent to act as if it is all another person's fault, instead of realizing they have the problem themselves. This often happens because they cannot identify the difference between their own issues and the issues of those on which they are dependent upon. Playing the role of a superhero entails looking very good on the outside. All of the giving is bound to start creating resentments within, even though saying yes feels good on the outside. It doesn't take long for other people to expect you to say yes. Part of the codependent feels indispensable, which makes people-pleasing reinforced. What happens is the codependent finds themselves saying, "I'm OK," instead of admitting to feeling overwhelmed. The tendency to ignore their own feelings becomes habit forming (bad habit, at that). It never occurs to the codependent to reach out for help, but the exhaustion starts to reveal itself in outbursts. The remedy for always being "fine" is the admission of feelings, admitting there is a need for change.

Obsessional thinking manufactured from the codependent's anxieties often creates a "fantasy land" within which they live. Incessant thoughts about how different things would be if their significant other(s) did not engage in harmful behaviors is a way for the codependent to escape the pain of the present circumstances. This situation usually leads to painful emotions, low self-worth, shame, and despair. A plethora of negative emotions is attached to rumination about fixing another person. Eventually, when ruminating hasn't fixed the problem, the person ultimately feels numb. Obsessive thinking by the codependent person is a defense mechanism for their painful emotions. Fantasizing and ruminating about how they are going to fix someone keeps them focused on the future and works as an escape from the present. The sad truth about this is, with their attempt to escape any unpleasant feelings, more unpleasant emotions are generated. Worry, in a sense, is a fantasy about what may happen, which in turn heightens the fear factor. The fear becomes distorted, virulent, and ends up as a toxic combination of the false belief that being human is a shameful state of being. This self-defeating and self-perpetuating type of obsessional thinking adds not only to the anxiety, but to further shaming because they believe that being afraid, itself, is shameful and weak.

Intimacy issues surround the codependent. Not referring to sex here; intimacy means feeling open, honest, and close with another. Due to weak boundaries, fear of rejection, and shame, the codependent struggles with the vulnerability necessary to feel intimate. The fear of intimacy goes hand in hand with the fear of abandonment, rejection, and betrayal. This usually stems from early childhood wounds. Sometimes a parent can threaten emotional abandonment if not getting the desired behavior from a child. A child is unable to see themselves as a separate entity from the parents. Hence, the parent's behavior lends itself to the development of self-worth in their children. Sharing who they are is extremely difficult for the codependent because, at their very core, there is a feeling of defectiveness and unworthiness. This is their defense mechanism against rejection and betrayal.

As long as the codependent continues to act subconsciously to their childhood trauma, they will repeat the pattern in their current families, risking a chance of passing the condition down from generation to generation. Since the codependent loses themselves in another due to blurred boundaries, they have a tremendous fear of being judged, which, in turn, closes them off and unable to provide true intimacy. The codependent is confused by the difference between intimacy and sex. They fear that, if they let go of themselves sexually, they might lose their autonomy. They fear being looked down upon by their lover or that they may lose respect. They do not view their sexual partners as being on equal terms. Even though codependents crave close bonds to ease their loneliness and pain, they are too busy caring for others and remain out of touch with what is going on within them, making intimacy nearly impossible.

Shame is also a central feature of codependency. It stems from being in a dysfunctional family since birth. Even though shame is a natural human phenomenon, most people will do anything necessary to avoid it. It is not just an emotion, it is a physiological response implemented by the autonomic nervous system similar to panic, with a rapid pulse, sweating, nausea, poor eye contact, and slumping shoulders all being features of shame. Shame is different from guilt, as shame is a feeling about yourself, whereas guilt is a judgment about whether you have behaved right or wrong. Guilt prompts you to correct an error or fix it. Shame on the other hand is an encapsulating feeling of inferiority, self-loathing, and inadequacy. You feel like hiding, or you feel humiliated, as if other people can outright see your flaws. The strong sense of isolation can be overwhelming.

Toxic shame can ruin a person's life and can cause terrible pain. Shame leaves the codependent with feelings of self-loathing, which is worsened by not being able to verbalize the emotion without further anxiety leading to more shame. Toxic shame is buried deep in the subconscious mind and many may be unaware they are suffering from it. The type of shame experienced by many codependent people has a long duration stemming from childhood. In fact, most codependent individuals have grown up feeling ashamed about their emotions, wants and needs. When grown, they deny their wants and devalue themselves in order to avoid intense feelings of shame. Just memories and thoughts can trigger immense feelings of shame; it does not have to be associated with an external event. Toxic shame spirals out of control, leaving the individual with feelings of despair, depression, and hopelessness. In a normal case scenario, shame leaves us shortly after an embarrassing incident, but the codependent has internalized shame, which is just waiting to be activated by some type of trigger. Internalized shame is often the root cause of low self-worth, leaving the codependent feeling unworthy, unhappy, and unlovable. The lack of ability in allowing oneself to experience positive emotions is caused by a constant repeating message in their mind that they are worthless. It plays like a looped cassette tape pushing the codependent to constantly crave control and tend to others in an effort to reduce those shameful emotions.

Generosity lies at the heart of the codependent—a sincere wish to ease another's suffering. It becomes very uncomfortable for the codependent to witness someone in pain. Helping is rewarding until the help stops working. The codependent thinks of themselves as a superhero because they continuously work to enable another without even breaking a sweat. However, on the inside, they may be getting sick and tired of it. The codependent keeps a smile going until bits of the frustration starts to leak out. All of a sudden, sarcasm without intent happens, and a loss of control over their feelings begins. They get to the point where it is increasingly easier to say yes when meaning no. Anger begins to build up as the superhero feels underappreciated. Craving recognition without asking for it sets up the significant others for confusion and resentment. The codependent "love" is exclusive to other people with little or none left for themselves. The codependent wants their love to be recognized, and so, as such, they may sound off a list of things they have done for someone. It is a conditional love, meaning they want something in return (i.e., what's the payback?). Those loved by the codependent are grateful on the outside, but there is always the underlying feeling of dishonesty or that the giver has some other agenda. This also breeds resentment in the recipients of the codependent. It also leads toward taking advantage of the codependent so as to "teach them a lesson". Often, a recipient of love from a codependent person wants to build up their supply because they do not feel it is genuine to begin with and, therefore, may be cut off at any moment.

People-pleasing is normally a component of low self-esteem in which the individual feels inadequate or unlovable and has to make sure they please people in order to feel validated. For the people-pleaser, saying the word "no" to someone creates severe anxiety. This person will often sacrifice their own needs to oblige other people. Codependent people are strongly motivated in seeking external validation and approval. This insecurity induces conformity to other people's expectations and opinions. They want to please others even when it is uncomfortable for them or it is something they, on the inside, really do not want to do. While people-pleasing, itself, is not a diagnosable mental illness, it is a strong component of the codependent condition. The codependent's people-pleasing can appear much like generosity; however, generosity comes from a genuinely happy feeling of shared enjoyment. For the codependent, people pleasing comes from a low self-worth and from *needing* the approval of others.

The codependent becomes subservient to others, lacking a balance of mutual respect. For many, the wish to please comes from self-worth issues. The codependent hopes that by saying yes to everything asked of them, that will help them feel accepted and liked. Other people-pleasers have a history of being badly treated. Sometime along the way, the pleasers decided that the best way that they can be treated better is to try to please the ones who treated them badly. Over time, people-pleasing became a way of life for them. Take note of the following seven signs of people pleasing:

1. **Pretending to agree with anyone and everyone.**
   Agreeing with someone just to be liked or out of fear of rejection can cause you to get involved in situations that go against your belief system and values.
2. **Feeling responsible for how others feel.** Thinking that you have the power to make someone else's life happy is a false reality. Everyone is the director of their own happiness. Some people have everything one could want except for happiness.
3. **Constantly apologizing and excessive self-blame** or

thinking you are always to blame is a symptom of a larger issue. You never need to be sorry for being you!

4. **You feel like your activities of daily living are a burden.** Since codependents are people-pleasers, most activities on their schedule are for someone else. It is very difficult for a person with codependency issues to meet their goals as they are busy helping other people meet theirs.

5. **Inability to say "no".** Sometimes the codependent will say yes when they mean no and then have to make up a fake excuse for why they 'can't' follow through with the plans they never wanted to make in the first place.

6. **Fear of another person being upset with you.** Just because someone else is upset doesn't necessarily mean that you did something wrong. Acting some kind of way because you simply can't handle the thought of someone being upset with you is akin to walking on eggshells.

7. **Trying to fit in by behaving the same as the people around you.** It is normal for different environments with different people in them to bring out different parts of your personality. But, the codependent will often get involved with self-destructive behaviors just to fit in, such as eating more than you wish at a friend's house so they are happy that you enjoyed their cooking.

Everyone *overreacts* to small happenings here and there, usually without realizing it. It is fine for a person to feel their emotions and sometimes get angry. However, the codependent expresses themselves in an unhealthy way. With this type of severe codependent style of overreacting, the person tends to lash out at anyone who pushes the right buttons. While this may, to some degree, be effective because you are standing up for yourself, it still comes out as crazy. This means the codependent is still soaking up other people's baggage and letting it affect them. The way anger is unleashed from the codependent is a good indication of being unstable. Serious problems begin to arise when overreacting, such as being at risk for injury from the person you verbally attacked. All the lashing out does is magnify the anxiety and fears of the codependent who is already worried about disapproval. Healthy individuals do their best to avoid overly reactive people because it is demoralizing. They are disinterested in the theatrical drama of the reactive person and will surely label them as unstable and not the type one wants to buddy up with. The more pain the codependent feels, the weaker their boundaries become and that reinforces the lashing out. The lashing out is a sign of external forces permeating the insides of the codependent.

People react to *triggers*, which are unique to each individual's personality and history. Triggers can be imagined as re-experiencing wounds from past traumas, but in the present time. The codependent often feels as if they do not measure up to someone else's standards, triggering shame. Activating the inner critic all of the time can ruin a person's life. A well-documented trigger for the codependent is repeatedly being told they are too sensitive and selfish. Given that they adopted this belief, the codependent will automatically offer assistance, even when it is harmful or counterproductive. When behaviors or feelings are magnified in intensity and duration, people, in general, overreact. If an external trigger brings up a bad experience from the past, overreactions can happen. For example, the war hero who hears fireworks and draws his gun, even though they are safely in their home. *Overreacting* is a symptom of a person lacking the ability to set boundaries. This is noticeable when an individual feels defensive when another disagrees with them or automatically believes to be true what the other thinks about them. The difference between good boundaries and poor boundaries is the realization that people have opinions that are not a reflection of one's self and, therefore, do not feel threatened.

People overreact when they absorb another person's words or feelings because there is no set boundary between the two. When anger cannot be managed, it becomes overwhelming. How individuals react is influenced by their inborn temperament and early childhood environment. Therefore, each individual's reactions are unique to their own personality. Some criticize, explode into rage, blame others, or say things they later regret. The codependent wants to avoid any conflict, so they hold their emotions in where they stockpile into resentments. But, like steam, anger builds up and always finds a way out. Codependents have learned very well how to employ passive-aggressive actions to relieve their anger buildup. For example, a codependent wife may be angry at her husband. Since, she fears verbalizing her feelings, she burns his dinner instead. If the aforementioned denial is in place, and the person doesn't allow themselves to feel or even take a mental note of their anger, and days, weeks, or years go by after the issues, a total meltdown can be in store. Anger can lead to illnesses because the stress related to the emotion wears a person's immune system down and the body's nervous system's ability to repair itself.

CODEPENDENCY AND THE NEED FOR CONTROL

Power plays a part in all relationships. It gives an individual a sense of control in their choices and their ability to influence others and the environment within which they live. It is a healthy and natural survival technique necessary for getting our needs met. Empowerment allows us to feel intrinsically involved in affecting outcomes and managing our emotions in the process. It puts us in a position of efficiency with an internal locus of control instead of overreacting. The codependent, in contrast, feels powerless and thinks they have fallen victim to outside forces. When not lashing out with a false sense of power, the codependent believes their destiny is in someone else's hands. Always acquiescing as to not sound mean, the codependent defers their needs and finds it difficult to make independent decisions. This impaired sense of power can stem from various elements common to codependents, such as low self-worth, shame, dependency, fear (both of rejection and abandonment), approval seeking, denial, and unreasonable expectations of other people coupled with their victim mentality. Most relationships known to the codependent have imbalances of power. With the difficulty they have in expressing their true feelings, it becomes natural for another to fill the void. In these relationships, sometimes a narcissist, alcoholic, addict, or abuser has power over the codependent person leading them to resort to passive-aggressive methods of trying to gain a sense of control. Over a period of time, the lack of power can ultimately cause depression and other physical problems.

In healthier relationships, if there is mutual respect, both individuals engage in ongoing power struggles. This usually revolves around time management, money, household chores, child-rearing techniques, and so on. In avoidance of conflict, some couples agree to separate domains of power. Traditionally, mothers tended to the children and the home, while fathers were the breadwinners. This continues very much today in many cultures, but is changing with the improved earning abilities of women, especially when also caring for young children (social evolution). In present times, men are much more involved in parenting, and women have more power outside of the home, teaching them they can easily function outside of the relationship. Feelings of resentment and imbalance are common issues that coincide with the changing times. This is why effective communication is so important so each partner can feel respected and powerful.

Decisions are made together with both partners assuming responsibility for the relationship and for themselves in a healthy couple scenario. This is where safety, values and needs are developed in a healthy relationship. Here, with shared power, each person wants to express their likes and dislikes, and what each will tolerate from the other. Sometimes, an individual is possibly feeling vulnerable from a lack of respect. The codependent has an impaired relationship with power; possibly coming from their submissive roles growing up where their feelings were criticized, and their needs ignored. Without the encouragement of self-worth and personal power, the codependent is left feeling as if love and power cannot coexist. They have learned the only way to exert power is indirectly. They might have learned that love is acquired only by acquiescing and pleasing others. Historically, this was common in families where girls were encouraged not to be assertive, educated, or self-reliant. The flip side of this is some children learn while growing up that the best way to meet their needs and feel safe is to have power over other people. When becoming an adult, this breeds fear and resentment in their partner, leading the partner into passive-aggressive actions to get their feelings acknowledged.

Many people with codependent personalities have never learned how to assertively solve problems. They very likely had a controlling parent. The codependent may end up rebelling and becoming authoritarian, themselves, which, again, is counterproductive to getting their needs met. They are unable to discern how to get their needs and wants met or how to make decisions for themselves. They give up control of their inner desires and turn to others or freeze (not act at all). Assertiveness requires self-esteem, which makes it difficult for the codependent as the lack of self-worth is one of the key components of the condition. Due to this lack of any sense of power within themselves, control and manipulation become part of the behavioral pattern in the codependent. They focus on external resources for happiness, instead of taking responsibility for their own. The codependent wants to get others to do things or act how they want them to in order to make themselves happy. When these expectations go unmet, the codependent falls into further despair and a further sense of powerlessness. People do not have to give up themselves to have love and power. Actually, love necessitates the exercise of power so we can show that we are responsible for our decisions. It takes power to directly ask for our wants and needs and to honestly express ourselves when setting healthy boundaries.

ROLES PLAYED BY THE CODEPENDENT

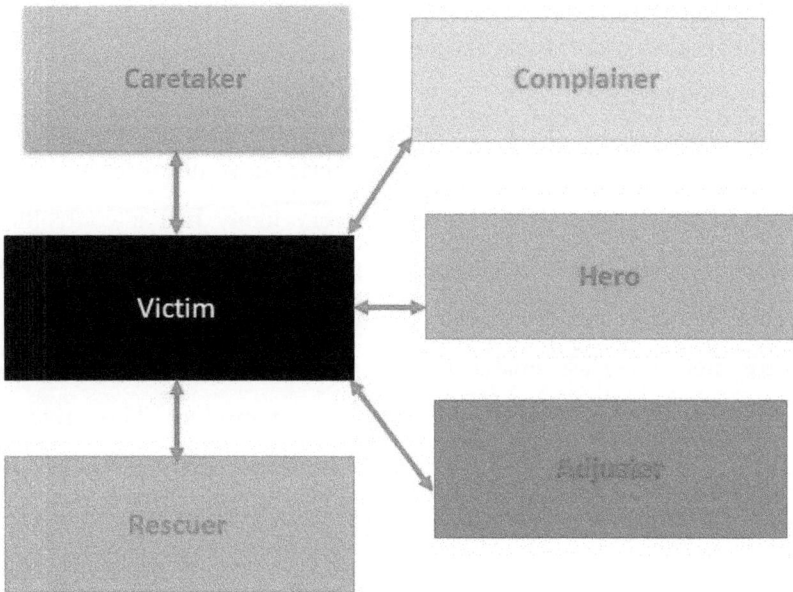

PREVALENCE OF CODEPENDENCY

It is difficult to establish how prevalent codependency is. Some suggest that, in the U.S., as much as 90% of the population demonstrates characteristics of codependency. The prevalence of codependency is difficult to ascertain partly because of its undetermined definition. Melody Beattie describes a codependent person as someone who allows another individual's behavior to affect them and who obsessively tries to control that person's behavior. Given the prevalence of codependency suggested by experts in the field of behavioral health, it is a condition that needs careful assessment and should not be overlooked when treating an individual, regardless of their presenting problem or any prior diagnosis. It is essential that anyone working in a therapeutic environment understand the characteristics of codependency well enough to have self-awareness of their own potential codependent traits. The severity and development of codependent characteristics overlap and vary. They derive from the codependents' lack of ability to tap into their inner core and primarily include:

- Painful emotions: Anxiety, hopelessness, sorrow, fear and despair;
- Denying that they are codependent and denying their emotions and feelings;
- Blurred or rigid boundaries;
- Poor communication skills; and
- Dependency on others.

When it comes to treating a client or offering expert advice, it is helpful to be able to remember that compulsive behaviors are prevalent in the personality of the codependent. The codependent thinks that they have to be codependent and have no choice in the matter. Even when the behaviors are self-destructive, the codependent will not cease to demonstrate them even when it is destroying their own lives. These individuals are commonly unhappy. They believe they can rescue the dependent person, making them better, when they are only reinforcing the dependency. Making matters even more serious is the belief that they will receive validation in return and when that doesn't happen, resentments start to flourish.

2

WHERE DOES CODEPENDENCY COME FROM?

Codependency most often stems from childhood to the relationships we had with our primary caretakers or parents. It usually occurs when one or both of the parents are under- or over-protective. When parents are overprotective, they restrain their child's autonomy and keep them from building the confidence necessary to go out into the world on their own. Normal anxieties include watching your child try new things, but forbidding them from trying stops them from learning how to complete basic tasks. When a parent or parents are under-protective, they do not provide their children with enough support and, therefore, they structure the basis of codependency. Missing this most important step in child rearing can leave the young one feeling unsafe and alone in the world (a breeding ground for anxiety and depression). Sometimes, a codependent parent will treat their son or daughter more like a friend, over-involving themself in their children's lives, living vicariously through them, and reinforcing dependent characteristics while discouraging them from becoming independent. When this happens, the codependent begins to harbor guilt for not wanting their child to have their own life. If a child grows up with a parent afflicted with alcoholism and/or drug addiction, the child or children stand the chance of being neglected or tending to the dependent parent and thus, the codependent child is launched.

One way codependency is passed down to children could be that it is "inherited" through genetics, which influences personality traits, such as empathy. Another type of inheritance is learning through observation. Children learn how to behave by watching someone model actions rather than learning it directly by experience. While researching the literature associated with codependency, studies noted that a parent's codependent actions, and what they explain to children about helping people, influences those children's behavioral characteristics into adulthood. If, when growing up, a child watches important people in their life over-help, enable and rescue, they become more prone to it themselves, especially when it is one of their parents, who are praised by others for how much they put up with. These behavioral traits are often taken in subconsciously when children are still too young to comprehend their negative consequences. Behaving in a codependent way becomes a habit despite its hazardous results. Professional help is usually necessary for identifying and breaking these patterns.

CODEPENDENT PARENTS

What if you are not in a healthy coupled relationship and are a codependent parent? A codependent parent has an unhealthy attachment to their child or children because they expect a degree of love and devotion to the point that it is destructive to the family as a whole. This usually occurs when the codependent parent is trying to make up for what was lacking in their own upbringing. A vicious cycle is happening, and decision-making processes are likely to become unhealthy because there are blurred boundaries between the parent and child. The message the child receives is one of, "I am not OK unless you are OK, or you tell me I am OK". In turn, the child or children of the codependent learn to pay close attention to the parent and ready themselves to act in a way that will not upset the parent. They don't per se want to 'rock the boat'.

A mother or father who is codependent has a difficult time effecting boundaries or imposing limits when a child misbehaves. So, the codependent parent loosens the rules and limitations so they can revert back to their normal emotional state. Sometimes, the codependent parent will toss their children's actions back at them, making it all about themselves. Due to the fact the parent's sense of who they are is dependent on the relationship they have with their child; they will possibly try to control every aspect of their children's life. If there are happenings in the life of their child that create a sense of anxiety in the codependent parent, the parent will try to gain control so as to provide relief to themselves by getting overly involved. The parent will literally do anything to gain control of their child so they can relieve their anxiety. Sometimes, the codependent parent will try to maintain control by telling their children of the difficult times they had as a child to try and garner sympathy.

Often when one or both of the parents are codependent, their relationship takes a back seat to the children, fearing the marriage or marital relationship will interfere with the parent-child relationship. This can come in the form of a subtle push-away so as to maintain the focus on the child or children. Even when the codependent caretaker is literally wrong, there will be no apology; if there is one it will be insincere, and noticeably so. When a codependent parent has a falling-out with a child, their authority feels threatened, or is viewed as the child acting out of rebellion. A common phrase said during this type of an interaction is, "I feel like I am talking to a brick wall!" A codependent parent will often use guilt as a weapon. Passive-aggression, such as the silent treatment or projecting blame, is often the chosen 'weapon' to use when a child is becoming autonomous. This can happen without the codependent parent even being aware of it. This is all put forth in an effort to control their child or children into doing as the parent forcefully suggests, especially when they are grown. This type of relationship between a parent and a child sets a premise for how a child will relate to life. Each experience a child has provides them with information about future decisions. Therefore, they are at a high risk of using the same dysfunctional behavioral patterns they have learned while growing up with a codependent parent when they become adults.

Family Boundaries

Family boundaries delineate who in the family is responsible for what. They create an emotional and a physical space between each member of the family. Boundaries are a safety net reflecting mutual respect for the feelings and the needs of each family member, while communicating clear roles and expectations. While growing up, a child's boundaries should shift gradually to allow for increased autonomy and privacy, allowing the young person to develop their own set of values and beliefs system. Codependency is a trait that is very helpful to children growing up in dysfunctional homes as they learn to navigate frightening and unpredictable family lives. However, these don't translate positively in adulthood. Enmeshment refers to a family system that has blurred boundaries and the expectations of the leaders of the family are confusing and inappropriate. When a parent relies on a child for support and, at the same time, the child is not allowed to be emotionally separate from their family members, they all become emotionally merged together in an unhealthy manner.

Common characteristics of an enmeshed family system:

- Blurred boundaries;
- Always about pleasing someone else;
- The family members feel responsible for their parents' happiness;
- The child is made to feel guilt and shame if they want a bit less contact with a parent;
- The parents' sense of worth depends on their children's successes;
- The parent **must** know everything about their children's life;
- The parents discourage their children from following their

dreams and goals, and imposing their own wishes on them is a must;

- The family shares private experiences too much with one another, and feelings are expressed in such a way that creates unhealthy dependence, unrealistic expectations and confused roles;

- The children feel that if they don't meet their parents' expectations, they will be emotionally abandoned or shamed; and

- The children begin to avoid discussions where they may have to say "No".

CODEPENDENCY AND SUBSTANCE ABUSE PATTERNS

* * *

LIVING WITH AN ADDICT

Addicts and alcoholics often rely on family members to supply their finances and to support their way of life. This is because their addiction has, in many cases, made them unable to take care of their basic necessities, such as a place to live, food, and money. They depend on the love of their family and want continuous validation of their love and support. Too often, family members feel the need to protect their afflicted so they can be a "good parent, spouse, sibling, friend, etc." The addict is sure of this, and they use it to get what they can and get away with it. Relationships function in give-and-take scenarios; they naturally affect one another. It is important to realize that the addict did not make a moral choice to be one. The addict is not necessarily a bad person, and it doesn't mean they don't love you. You did not cause their addiction, either, and you cannot change it or control it. You can still have compassion for the addict without enabling them in order for you to feel like a good person. Like the addict, the codependent does not have a flawed personality and is not a moral failure. To help you to understand how to start the healing process, you must first know the normal effects of relationships. Relationships connect people in one or more of the following ways:

- An individual will assume some of the qualities of the other.
- An individual will assume a position that complements the qualities of the other.
- An individual will assume a position counteracting the qualities of the other.

The most important thing to understand about these scenarios is that the connection between two people in a relationship changes the people. Everyone is changed as a result of a connection to a person who is addicted to a substance. To help you to understand codependency with an addict, use the same scenarios above, but change a few words.

- An individual will assume some of the *unhealthy* qualities of the addict or alcoholic.
- An individual will assume a position that complements the *unhealthy* qualities of the addict or alcoholic.

- An individual will assume a position counteracting the *unhealthy* qualities of the addict or alcoholic.

To arrive at the next step, replace the word individual with you, and then replace the words addict and alcoholic with the name of your addicted friend or loved one. Addicts often avoid seeking treatment, and so do codependents. It is an uncomfortable process for both. For change to happen, the discomfort must be faced. Thankfully, the discomfort is not permanent as it is just a time of transition. If an alcoholic or addict could stop on their own, they would certainly have done so long before many of the common and serious negative consequences had come along. Actually, when an intervention is accomplished with an addict or alcoholic, it is the first move toward change for the codependent. Difficult at first, the uncomfortable times are well worth the benefits in the long-term and often lifesaving for both. If you are involved with an addict, know it is your partner with the addiction, yet if codependent, you are the one putting a huge amount of pressure on yourself to solve the problem, as if it is your responsibility to restore their sanity. This again stems from abandonment fears and low self-esteem. Unfortunately, the help you are attempting to offer is only hurting the addict in the long run. If the addict does not take the first step by admitting they have a problem with drugs and/or alcohol, their chances of sobriety will be low, to say the least.

When a person with whom you are involved is addicted, they may become hostile and defensive when you attempt to help. Try not to take it personally. It is the codependent's low self-worth that makes it seemingly impossible to understand things from this perspective. Even when you know your partner is sick, you will still feel devastated by their harsh behavior and their rejection of your help. A classic component of codependency is the constant seeking of the partner's affirmation because you depend on that in order for you to feel good about yourself. This is an unhealthy behavior under any circumstance. When your loved one is dealing with addiction, the last thing they need is someone afraid to confront the problem. They do, however, need honesty, which is what you struggle with when letting your codependency stay in control. The love and compassion you feel for someone so close to you are obvious under these brutal circumstances, but your need to keep your abandonment fears at bay can actually lengthen the misery already in place. Commonly, the codependent will become obsessed with trying to fix the addict often to the point of neglecting their own needs.

Addicts can often be extremely verbally abusive and frequently lie to their significant others. The codependent is the one left to clean up their messes. Now is when the one involved with the addict should refuse immediately and let them know this is an unacceptable behavior. But, if codependent, you are probably going to refuse to do what is best, and subject yourself to more abuse while helping them to keep using. Of course, people who abuse alcohol or drugs need help and advice from their loved ones, but in the case of codependency, the efforts made for help are overbearing to the point of acting parental toward the addict as if they are a small child incapable of doing anything on their own. If it gets to this point, you are attempting too hard to control the situation. This is ineffective and may trigger the addict's self-defensive tendencies; a consequence of codependency. Codependents commonly resort to manipulating others to get what they want, using shame, guilt, and embarrassment to play on their emotions. This method ultimately does not get the desired results. Entering treatment just to satisfy the codependent will not be successful. No matter how often you attempt to control the addict's behavior and how your relationship progresses, you are left feeling vulnerable and powerless. Overwhelming fears and feelings of helplessness set in and finally you become convinced that you are trapped. This, in turn, makes for a more unpredictable and uncertain future. As the patterns continue, the codependent may start to lie or blame others for their situations, making it easier for them not to face the consequences of their behavior and remain in a state of denial. Here lies the foremost example of codependency: enabling.

When someone you love is struggling with drug or alcohol addiction, you and other people close to that individual can be of great importance in helping the individual to overcome their addiction and to provide the motivation and emotional support needed to help them with their recovery. This is, of course, provided that the individual is ready to enter treatment necessary for the recovery process. However, codependent relationships have the directly opposite effect, increasing the chances that the person will either never seek treatment or, even after seeking treatment, relapse. It is a lose-lose situation for both the addict and the codependent because it makes it harder for the addict to stop. Enabling makes it challenging for the addict to stick to their treatment goals, unfortunately ending in relapse and a return to self-destructive actions.

For the codependent struggling in a relationship with an addict, both people may go through many negative consequences based on the problem. Some of these potential consequences include:

- Potential for also developing substance, food, sex, shopping or gambling addictions.
- Loss of friends and family relationships with people outside of the codependent relationship.
- Failure to meet responsibilities outside of the codependent relationship.

You have more power than you think you do. Even though you can't cure someone else, or make all their decisions for them, even if you are working with their best interest at heart; what you CAN control are the choices you make and the boundaries that you set in place. In general, codependents work so hard to rescue their addicted counterpart that they end up getting sick themselves. Partners and family members of addicts often struggle with the thought that they cannot help their loved one. A sense of "failing" their loved one can create a vicious cycle of shame, guilt, fear, resentment, and more (see the CoDA five patterns).

EMPATHY

Empathy is the ability to understand, realize and share the feelings and thoughts of another human being, animal, or some fictional character read in a book or viewed in a movie. Some who feel high degrees of empathy may think of themselves as 'highly sensitive', meaning their emotions are affected by the energy of people in their surroundings. It is like walking into an office after the boss 'reamed out' a coworker, and you can feel the tension in the room. It is imperative for people to develop empathy so they can establish relationships and provide compassion. It allows us to help other people by experiencing their point of view, and it comes from within and without being forced. It is important because it enables us to connect to others. It may have originally evolved for survival purposes both when we needed help or detected danger. If you think about a baby, maybe 2 years old, you will notice that they have the sincere ability to try and comfort a parent.

The ability to show support for a friend or loved one is an important part of building positive relationships. It allows us to have rapport with others, making them feel understood. Showing you understand another's perspective further cements the connections we make in life. In present days, external validation is no longer an evolutionary means of surviving, but for many, it still feels like it. The fine line is that, when you put yourself in someone else's shoes, if not careful, it can make you vulnerable and blind to your own needs. Some people will take advantage of your empathy if you are not sensitive to the warning signs. If you put the perspectives and emotions of others above your own, emptiness can set in, and the chance of developing anxiety and depression can arise. The difference between codependency and empathy is that one who feels empathy has a solid sense of who they are without taking other people's emotions personally, or feeling an uncontrollable urge to fix or change them. Each individual is meant to experience their own unique journey in life; even when times of feeling misunderstood occur, we realize it is not evidence of who we are. When others are experiencing emotional circumstances, empathy gives us the ability to give a person our undivided attention by listening and being fully present. If codependency exists, there is an immediate reaction to instantly fix the person with solutions for their problems. The codependent reacts this way because the emotions of the other person at the time are absorbed and are intolerable. The consequences of these self-centered reactions lead the person with the problem to feel unheard (of course, the best intentions were at hand by the codependent). Being truly empathetic means having defined boundaries around what we will accept and what we will not. It gives us an understanding of why a person does a particular thing while also holding *them* responsible for their own actions. Empathy enables us in the understanding that each unique individual has their own version of the truth and that it is out of place for us to enforce our version of the truth on others.

Empathy differs from compassion, but they are closely related. Compassion is how we respond emotionally to sympathy, and it triggers a desire to help. Empathy is an awareness of another individual's emotions while attempting to understand how they feel. There is also a very fine line between being codependent and being a loving/caring person. If you hit the label "codependent" on the human being's empathetic and kind character traits, we might as well label all of the great spiritual icons, such as Mother Theresa and Buddha as codependents beyond repair. Kindness—far from a synonym of codependent—comes from a spiritual or humanitarian place inside each of us (or most of us). It takes perceptiveness to identify codependency from the human characteristics of love and compassion. Nurturing and supporting others provides us with a reward of feeling 'warm and fuzzy'. The world can always use a bit more sensitivity and compassion. A central component of love is noticing other people's needs, and if possible, providing it to them without overextending yourself; keeping a vital balance of caring for yourself while caring for others is key to keeping sane. We have to be careful about casually throwing around the codependent label, as we may miss the fact that we are complex individuals motivated by many incentives. It is a disservice to neglect ourselves in favor of attending to the needs of others. Working diligently to avoid being labeled codependent creates obstacles toward having healthy connections and intimate relations with others.

There is such a thing as *empathy fatigue,* as in having too much empathy. It can be harmful to your health. Leading with the heart and not the head can lead to making poor decisions when in a relationship. You do not want to lose perspective about what is best for you. There are several central elements to finding harmony in your life and reducing any negativity. How about the basics—exercise, hydration, sleep, and nourishment—without which is a state of unhappiness. Here is the key: you have to nurture your mind and spirit, as well. Nourishing your spirit with gratitude creates a barrier against negative emotions that can be destructive to your happiness. It is impossible to feel resentment, envy, anger, and regret while feeling grateful at the same time. They are not compatible with one another. Gratitude is an action word and allows you to actively participate in your life; it tends to magnify the good things.

IS CODEPENDENCY A MENTAL ILLNESS?

The extent to which codependency exists on its own is a subject for debate, with some people feeling it is a disorder severe enough to be categorized in the Diagnostic and Statistical Manual of Mental Disorders, 5th Edition (DSM-5), while others think it is a symptom of other disorders with no scientific research supporting the concept of codependency. The DSM-5 gives a comprehensive foundation for classifications and symptoms of conditions related to behavioral health. As early as 1986, experts in the field of behavioral health contended that codependency should be officially recognized as a mental health condition with diagnostic criteria shared from other disorders, including borderline personality disorder (BPD), histrionic personality disorder, dependent personality disorder (DPD), and even post-traumatic stress disorder (PTSD), qualifying that it has a recognizable personality disorder worthy of placement in the DSM-5.

The DSM-5 does not include codependency; however, it does include DPD. The reasoning behind not including codependency in the DSM-5 is that it has too much in common with other diagnoses causing an overlap to the extent that it does not merit its own place. However, newer studies revealed that, even though codependency overlaps a good deal with BPD and DPD, there are symptoms that are not included in either. This proposes codependency as a unique mental health condition. DPD shares the most in common with Codependency. The main difference is the way they behave in relationships. While DPD refers to individuals who show dependent characteristics toward other people in general, the codependent shows dependent characteristics on a specific individual. Likewise, an individual with BPD has difficulty with maintaining stability in relationships in general and the codependent involves a specified dependence on an individual.

Given the similarities between the condition of codependency and the DSM-5 criterion for DPD, it is noted that the main difference is in the degree of functionality of both the role as a codependent and the enabler role. Once identified, and codependency has been ruled out of the differential criterion, the attributing problems to problematic relationships are considered as relative characteristics of codependency. Currently, codependency is only considered a condition, psychological in nature, where an individual feels a dependence for a certain significant other in an extreme fashion. It is a distorted perspective of one's self that influences every action, behavior, anything said and one's complete path in life, essentially living as only one-half of a person that thinks they are responsible for the feelings and actions of another, eventually leading to low self-worth.

Once more, if the cycle is uninterrupted, the codependent is doomed to passing the condition onto the next generation. The way we interact and relate to people who are significant in our lives determines the degree of enjoyment and pain experienced in life. In the best-case scenario, the people around us are hopefully there to aid us in achieving our full potential. They are there for encouragement, support, and to help us follow our dreams. On the flip side of the best-case scenario coin, we are there to lift them up when they are down and care for them during a crisis. Here lies the dilemma of not getting so caught up in their problems that you are consumed by them.

* * *

QUESTIONNAIRE: ARE YOU A CODEPENDENT?

Answer the following questions and give yourself a score of 1 for each "yes" answer:

1. Do you try to get approval from others by rescuing, tending to their needs and then feeling disappointment when you are not validated?

YES	NO

2. Do you spend your spare time feeling anxious about other people or about doing something for someone else because you fear being alone?

YES	NO

3. Have you ever been in an abusive relationship and stayed when you knew you shouldn't?

YES	NO

4. Was the family you were raised in dysfunctional?

YES	NO

5. Have you ever been emotionally, physically or sexually abused?

YES	NO

6. Was either one of your parents codependent or narcissistic?

YES	NO

7. Is there any type of addiction in your family background?

YES	NO

8. Do you tell people too much about yourself before you get to know them very well?

YES	NO

9. Do you care more about what other people think about you than you think about your own well-being?

YES   NO

10. Does your personal history include many troubled relationships?

YES   NO

11. Do you have low self-worth and suffer from shame?

YES   NO

12. Have you ever lied to get someone else off the hook?

YES   NO

13. Has anyone ever suggested you are overactive?

YES   NO

14. Have you ever dated a narcissist?

| YES | NO |

15. Do you say "yes" when you mean "no"?

| YES | NO |

16. Do you believe you did not matter when growing up?

| YES | NO |

17. Do you have problems setting boundaries?

| YES | NO |

18. Have you ever enabled someone to continue drinking or drugging in spite of the consequences?

| YES | NO |

19. Do you try to go above and beyond to make someone else happy before you feel happy yourself?

YES	NO

20. Have any of your relationships caused you to lose sleep at night?

YES	NO

Now add up your score here _____.

(See Suggested Recommendations in Appendix 1).

3

WHAT DOES CODEPENDENCY LOOK LIKE?

Codependence is a condition that decays the spirit and freedom of those who suffer in dysfunctional relationships and families. It affects the lives of their families, friends, professional careers, their health, and their spirituality. It drains the person of all they have and, if left without seeking help, causes them to become more self-destructive and destructive to others. Some codependents are pushed by friends, therapists, colleagues, or other family members to get help. Codependency occurs when individuals live in the extremes of drama and lack balance in their lives. Often their partners, friends, and families are affected by the dysfunctional control characteristics the codependent portrays, all under the disguise of helping.

There are many roles occupied by the codependent:

1. Victim: Unfortunately, playing the victim role rarely works to the advantage of the codependent. It actually pushes partners, family members, co-workers, and friends away. The following are signs of playing the victim:

- Refusing to take responsibility for their own circumstances; it is always someone else causing the problem, oftentimes pointing the finger in an attempt to make someone feel guilty.
- Often when the codependent is in the victim role, they are paralyzed with fear and believe they are at the mercy of their partner. They feel powerless in this role and, as a result, stop growing.
- When in the victim role, the codependent spurs resentments, holding on to old injustices and manipulating others to feel badly about their behavior. Bringing up past negative memories and excuses as to why they cannot get out of their dysfunctional relationships is the hallmark of the victim role.
- The codependent lacks assertiveness skills when playing the victim and sincerely doubts they have control in their life; therefore, it becomes challenging for them to verbalize their needs, wants, and desires, and they usually remain in a looping pattern of submissiveness. This leads to low self-esteem, anxiety, panic attacks, and depression.

2. Rescuer/Hero: In the case of the codependent and the addict or alcoholic, it is not uncommon for the codependent to literally put the addict in bed after they pass out from over-imbibing.

- "Somebody help me...Everybody help me" is the phrase that ignites the entire realm of stress hormones in the codependent, along with a powerful need to connect to others in the only way they have ever known how. Most are familiar with this role. It is your motherly friend who takes in all of the stray animals and religiously does their partner's dirty laundry. It is the fierce soldier who goes to war every day to save "anything that needs saving". Guilt is not the motivating factor here; rather it is the intense need to be needed. The codependent relies on the rescuer role to give them some sense of self. The codependent needs to rescue more than whomever needs rescuing, in most cases.

- The codependent often feels a drop in self-esteem when there are lags in time between rescues. There is an unsettled feeling that there is something terribly wrong with the situation and the codependent person marches toward finding the next person who needs rescuing.

- The rescuer usually seems to be on a mission to commit to addicts or others whose lives are unmanageable. They always need some form of rescue whether it be in the form of sympathy, money, or an alibi.

- The rescuer role usually develops early in life when feelings of powerlessness were being developed. Imagine a young child who is put in a position of having to rescue their mother or father, siblings, or the entire family. This family is prone to have a big "I can't" as a common phrase in their household. Over time, this rescuer role becomes so embedded in the person that it is the only method they know when it comes to connecting to other people. Unfortunately, this young person has learned that the only way to meet their own needs is by living vicariously through meeting the needs of others. Therefore, in adult life, the codependent searches for what is familiar.

- The codependent in the rescuer role often views themselves as heroically saving the family image.

3. Caretaker: The codependent caretaker embodies the role of maid, parent, sex slave, chef, accountant, banker, nurse, etc. Everyone feels a certain amount of desire to be needed, but the codependent in this role takes it to the extreme. Caretaking to the extreme can be harmful to your partner and self-destructive to you. In this role, the codependent loses their identity and basically smothers their partner, leaving them no time or room to work on solving their own problems. In the dysfunctional family, as previously mentioned, the codependent learns from an early age that if not needed, they have no value whatsoever. Hence, the caretaker is completely dependent on their partner to be needed.

4. Joiner: The codependent often wants to imagine their partner's dysfunctional characteristics as being normal by simply permitting the unhealthy behaviors and sometimes joining them in their unhealthy actions, such as taking drugs, gambling, or excessive drinking. When in the role of the joiner, the codependent may regularly stop by the store on the way home from work and buy some alcohol, such as a bottle of wine, and have two glasses ready for their addicted partner by the time they come home. Also, they may make sure that the alcohol or drug is in full supply so there is no chance of withdrawals.

5. Complainer: In this role, the codependent incessantly blames others for all their problems. It is part of their delusional thinking patterns. After developing resentment, anger, loneliness, and bitterness, they will complain about how underappreciated they are when they have done so much to help. The codependent will constantly complain without ever finding any type of solution. This makes them uncomfortable to be around, but the codependent doesn't care. They are trapped in the loop of thinking if they complain enough, something will change, but it never does.

6. Adjuster: The individual tries to become invisible. The codependent repeatedly adjusts their behavior to avoid abandonment or rejection. They use fantasy to escape reality and tend to deny having any feelings at times.

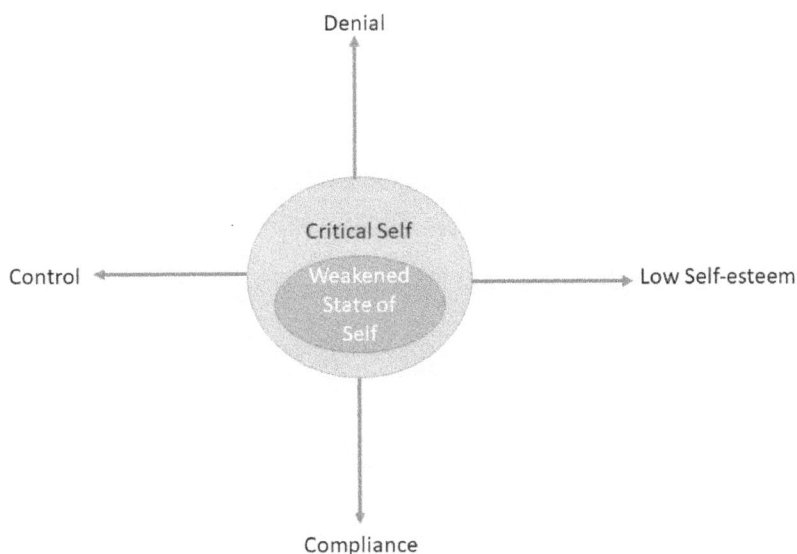

Denial

Critical Self

Control ← → Low Self-esteem

Weakened State of Self

Compliance

As previously discussed, a codependent feels responsible for the actions, feelings and behaviors of someone else without practicing self-perseverance. It takes two to take part in a relationship, and the people-pleaser/rescuer personality, unfortunately, is a perfect complement for someone who is completely self-serving. The signs of codependency have been listed in five patterns identified by Co-Dependents Anonymous (CoDA, 2020):

1. Denial Pattern

- Minimize or deny their true feelings.
- See themselves as totally unselfish and committed to the well-being of others.
- Lack of empathy for others' feelings.
- Project their own negative traits onto others.
- They believe they need no help from others.
- Mask their pain with anger, humor, or isolation.
- Verbalize negativity in indirect and passive-aggressive ways.
- Do not recognize how emotionally unavailable the people to whom they are attracted are.
- Struggle with identifying feelings.

2. Low Self-Esteem Pattern

- Indecisiveness.
- Judge themselves harshly, as never being good enough.
- Feel embarrassed when receiving praise or recognition.
- Place extreme value on the approval of others, on the way they think, feel, and behave.

- Think they are not lovable.
- Low self-worth.
- Seek approval to overcome feelings of worthlessness.
- Struggle with admitting a mistake.
- Think of themselves as being superior to others.
- Depend on others for a sense of safety.
- Struggle with procrastination.

3. Compliance Pattern

- Stay in destructive situations too long because of extreme loyalty.
- Compromise their own integrity and values out of fear of rejection or anger.
- Don't do what they want; just do what others want.
- Overly sensitive about the feelings of others and incorporate those feelings into their own psyche.
- Fear of expressing their own opinions, emotions, and beliefs if they are different from those around them.
- Accept sexual relationships when they want love.
- Have little regard for consequences when making decisions.
- In order to gain approval from others or to avoid any type of change, they are willing to give up their own truth.

4. Control Patterns

- Have the belief that individuals are incapable of caring for themselves.

- Manipulate or try to convince others on how to feel, what to think and do.
- Frequently give direction and advice without solicitation.
- When their help is refused, they become resentful.
- Shower gifts and services on people they want to influence.
- Use sex to manipulate or gain acceptance or approval.
- Being needed is a must in order to be involved in a relationship.
- Demand others meet their needs.
- Use their charisma and charm to show others they are compassionate and caring.
- Blame and shame to emotionally exploit others.
- Will not compromise, cooperate, or debate.
- Behave helplessly, indifferently, authoritatively, or angrily to manipulate results.
- Use twelve-step slogans in attempts to exert control over the way others behave.
- Falsely act in agreement with others to achieve what they want.

5. Avoidance Pattern

- Elicit shame, anger, and rejection through behaving in such a way.
- Criticize others' thoughts and actions.
- Avoid intimacy in a sexual, emotional, and physical way to maintain distance.

- Permit people, places, and things to become addictions blocking the development of intimacy in relationships.
- Skirt issues when communicating to avoid confrontation or conflict.
- Refuse help of any kind or participation in recovery.
- Repress their thoughts, needs, and feelings to circumvent feeling vulnerable.
- Draw people close only to push them away.
- Have the belief that if you show emotions you are weak.
- Rarely show signs of appreciation.

INTIMACY PROBLEMS

Emotional and physical intimacy with others is often a problem for the codependent. They have a strong tendency to fear judgment and rejection, needing to always appear all-powerful, helpful, and strong. Also referred to as intimacy avoidance, the fear of intimacy by the codependent is characterized as an anxiety around sharing a close physical or emotional relationship with another. It is not that the codependent wants to avoid being intimate, and may even wish for connectedness, but usually pushes their partner away or even sabotages the relationship. Intimacy avoidance can be rooted in several causes, such as a dysfunctional family system of origin, a history of emotional and/or physical abuse, and many other prevalent factors portrayed in the codependent. Conquering intimacy anxiety can take time necessary for exploring and understanding the issues that have contributed to it and for learning how to allow greater vulnerability.

Codependents with fear of loss or abandonment, along with a fear of engulfment are at the center of intimacy avoidance. Rooted in childhood experiences, the codependent is often confused by their reactions to present-day adult relationships. Fear of engulfment is where great anxiety is associated with control, domination, or identity loss in a relationship and can be rooted in enmeshed family dynamics. The fear of engulfment differs from the fear of abandonment in that it is usually rooted in overprotective parenting. Sometimes this may be a parent who seems very generous and loving on the surface but is also overly involved and controlling in their children's lives by not giving them the chance to develop their own unique perspectives in life, which is a vital part of development. There is a severe lack of boundaries in the relationship between child and parent. When a child's individuality is compromised and their identity ignored, narcissism and selfish traits may develop to institute a false sense of self and to assist them in meeting their needs. When fear of engulfment is present, the codependent worries about being smothered and, therefore, becomes very uncomfortable when in intimate situations. The fear of engulfment or of being invaded is characterized by distorted thoughts about losing oneself or being controlled. The codependent has learned to respond to conflict with controlling behaviors that vary from rage and blame, to acquiescence, resistance, and withdrawal. If one of the partners needs some alone time, the codependent feels rejected, abandoned and judged, which triggers other dysfunctional behaviors, including shame, guilt, depression, and panic. When the fear of engulfment and rejection becomes too much, the codependent may decide it is far too painful to have any intimacy at all. It is important to note that the codependent may engage in sexual activity as an obligation or to reinforce their desire to be needed. This leads to a lack of emotional growth, and the cycle is bound to repeat itself.

FEARING REJECTION

There is no doubt that rejection is painful. It is human nature to want to be connected with others and to belong. Feeling rejected by important people in your life and believing you are not wanted is an awful experience. It can seem at times to be physically painful. After experiencing the repeated trauma of rejection as a child, it is no wonder why the codependent wants to avoid ever feeling that way again. The fear of rejection holds many back from achieving success in their lives but can actually overcome it with a bit of work. Most experience rejection over both big and small issues at times in their lives, such as:

- Being ignored when asking a friend to hang out.
- Not receiving an invitation to an event that many people you know are attending.
- Being cheated on in a relationship.

Rejection is painful no matter what the source is. The codependent usually has a higher degree of sensitivity to rejection and feels wounded when others see the incidents in their lives as no big deal. Rejection includes other painful emotions, such as shame, embarrassment, and awkwardness. The first step in allaying your fear of rejection is by acknowledging it. Denying that you're hurt when you really are takes away your chance of productively conquering your fear. While it may not seem so at first, rejection can actually provide you with the opportunity for growth and self-discovery. For instance, you applied for a position in a company that you really want and thought your interview went fantastically, and then you don't get the job. So, you brush over your resume and realize you may need to add to your professional toolkit by learning new types of computer software (the ole 'silver lining in the cloud'). After a couple of months, you now see that many new doors have now opened due to your new learned skills qualifying you for even higher-paying positions. Turning your fear of rejection into an opportunity for growth can boost your ability in trying to get what you want while easing the pain of failure. Try thinking that you will learn a lesson, from the failure, which will benefit you later on.

Codependents heighten their fears of rejection by reading too much into it. Feeling unworthy of love, coupled with a lack of self-confidence creates a sort of paralysis in the individual, leading them to be too fearful of changing themselves for the better. Always imagining the worst-case scenarios or 'waiting for the other shoe to drop' can lead to a very sickly way of living. It has a snowball effect that can make it seem impossible to ever become somehow stable. This cycle of negative thinking spirals into a behavior known as *catastrophizing*. It is usually based on an unrealistic fear.

Catastrophizing is when you always think the worst possible scenarios will happen. It often includes the belief that the situation you are in is worse than it really is and that the challenges you face are more difficult than they really are. For example, you may worry that you are failing in your relationship, and from there you may assume failing in this relationship means failure for any future relationships

WHAT DOES CODEPENDENCY LOOK LIKE? | 75

and that you are a bad person. Many people's relationships fail, but it is not proof that you will not be able to recover. By catastrophizing, you may not have the ability to acknowledge that. The difference between catastrophizing and over-exaggeration is that catastrophizing is usually not intentional or that simple. People usually don't even realize they're doing it because it has become such a habit. It can even affect an individual's health.

CYCLE OF CODEPENDENCY

Codependents often have good intentions while perpetuating this cycle. They want to take care of a loved one who is experiencing difficulties (substance abuse, mental illness) and do this by 'covering' for them, making excuses, working to reduce consequences from action or inaction, etc. However, these attempts to help their loved one actually have the opposite effect in the long run. The needy individual continues on their destructive path with no incentive to change, as they rely on the codependent to take care of everything. The more needy the individual becomes, the more the codependent feels they are getting a reward and validation from being needed (often subconsciously). After some time, the caretaking reaches a point where it is compulsive, and the codependent feels trapped and helpless while simultaneously feeding into the cycle of behavior. Codependency is a symptom of the S.A.D. (Seduce-Abuse-Discard) cycle functioning in the background.

Seduction phase

During the seduction phase of the S.A.D. cycle, the narcissist or taker (similar to a parasite) targets a codependent to add to their supply of ego inflators. The supply will include anything the codependent has that the taker desires, such as money, status, good looks, culinary skills, attention, and sex. One of the key components to this part of the cycle is the amount of attention the codependent receives while being lavished, praised, and having time spent on them. This provides a sense of euphoria within the codependent because it mirrors their internal fantasy of being loved. In their grandiosity, the taker may say the codependent completes them, and that they are exactly what the taker has been looking for (i.e., "You are my soulmate!"). (Notice the term *what* they have been looking for, not *who*). The taker wants what they want, and they want it NOW! Early marriage proposals, wanting to move in with each other, wanting to spend every minute of the day together; before long... "Darn, I had a really tight month financially, do you think you can help me out, and could I maybe stay at your place?" This is a prime example of enmeshment with goal being entrapment. Here is where the codependent begins to lose their identity.

Abuse Phase

The abuse phase of the S.A.D. cycle is where the taker's use of the codependent starts to become abuse. They no longer feel such ego inflation from conquering their prey; the rush is over, and now they start becoming easily annoyed. The codependent is now committed and has become increasingly emotionally dependent and obsessed with fixing any problems. The taker becomes secure enough to reveal who and what they really are. This is awfully confusing to the code-pendent, who turns to their inner belief that they were not good enough. The codependent starts to try and change themselves to fit the taker's wants, hoping to resume the seduction phase. This phase of the cycle triggers the codependent's abandonment fears and validates their feelings of unworthiness. Here, the fixer or rescuer begins to take charge. One goal the taker has during the abuser phase is to increase their control over the codependent; the more worn down they are, the easier they will be to control. The more abuse, the more shame the codependent feels, deepening their feelings of inadequacy. The codependent simply tries even harder to fix the taker, fix them-selves, and delve deeper into their fantasy that the taker truly loves them, but is just having difficulty showing it. The taker uses their narcissistic skill set and plays into the situation by:

- Blaming the codependent;
- Attempting to make the codependent question their reality;
- Verbally abusing, e.g., "You are a wussy!";
- Attacking the codependent's character;
- Making the codependent the villain;
- Denying accountability;
- Making false promises;
- ...and the list goes on.

The Discard Phase

The biggest fear a codependent has is to be discarded. It causes a feeling of paralysis, turning into submissiveness. Abandonment threats trigger a deeper feeling of shame and powerlessness. This is in line with the same element that gives the codependent that feeling of euphoria during the seduction phase, as well as the stress and sorrow during the abuse phase. Codependents feel as if they will not survive abandonment by their significant other. This comes from the trauma of childhood emotional and/or physical abandonment. This awful feeling of incompleteness and isolation looks to the taker for wholeness and completion. The natural process of individuation when a child learns they are separate and unique to their parents was impaired. Now that the codependent thinks they have met a person who 'really' cares and gave them all of that praise in the seduction phase, their dysfunctional childhood is reactivated. During the discard phase, all of the love and care is taken back, often quickly, and the codependent is sent spiraling into despair and emotional isolation. However, the act of discarding the codependent is not always permanent. Sadly, the codependent can be wooed back within minutes to the seduction phase.

In the discard phase, the untreated codependent can fall into self-pity. Most individuals have at least one person they know whose main topic of conversation is themselves. Hearing someone say, "Woe is me" all the time can drain everyone they are around of their energy and happiness. Attention-seeking and condolence-craving are the primary symptoms of the codependent in the discard phase. For some reason, the codependent feels some sense of relief from their sense of victimhood. It is associated indistinguishably with their patterns of behavior linked to their growing-up years. When focusing on what you think to be fair in life and feeling confident that your situation is worse than anyone else's, you are drowning in self-pity. This can be a complete 'turnoff' to those around you. The sense that you are always being slighted shows in your body posture and facial expressions without even having to verbalize your feelings. If somewhere in your mind you believe that your self-pity will keep you from being discarded, you can't be any further from reality. No one wants to be around a frowning person. Low self-worth and depression are quick to follow. Isolation will become prominent as you will slowly have to come to terms with the fact that a change is necessary.

Always venting how pitiful your life seems to your partner or other significant people in your life, rather than taking action to improve your situation, will put you in a state of mental weakness, and it is also unattractive. There is a saying in the Twelve-Step philosophy: "Accept the things you cannot change (Bill W., 1939)". Not every problem in life has a solution; hurricanes still come, loved ones still pass away, but the key to keeping a healthy mental state is acceptance, not self-pity. At some point in each individual's life, tragedy happens. Knowing you will survive and grow under any conditions is what getting better is all about. Mental toughness requires keeping self-pity at a minimum. No one ever said life is easy, everyone is taking the mental, physical, and spiritual journey together. There is a myriad of good examples out there of ways to triumph during tough times, so how long you suffer depends on you, even though it may not seem like it at the time. There are those who stay comfortable in their grief and never seem to be able to rebuild, and unfortunately after being discarded, find themselves in another abusive codependent relationship. Self-pity gives you a reason to not even attempt to conquer your goals. The difference between a healthy mind and one dwelling in misery is that the mentally fit person sees others and their accomplishments as an inspiration rather than those minds dwelling in the misery of envy.

THE DYSFUNCTION DANCE: CODEPENDENT VS. NARCISSIST

The dysfunctional-codependent-versus-narcissist dance requires two opposing personality types but an inherently balanced duo: the codependent rescuer/fixer and the narcissist/taker. It is tough to say, but the truth is that those suffering from codependency often find themselves wrapped up in a torrid relationship with a narcissist. Narcissists are comforted by the term codependence by feeling admirable for not being one. A narcissist is a person who is so excessively self-involved that their desires trump anyone else's with whom they are involved. Some of the characteristics of a narcissist include: entitlement, a lack of empathy, and compassion. Ironically, while codependency and narcissism are often thought of as opposite, there are similar behavioral traits in both. Some of these include blurred boundaries, the need to control or depend on others for validation, and denial. Really the only difference between narcissism and codependency is the narcissist's lack of empathy and sense of entitlement.

Codependents and narcissists both can be seemingly charming, warm, and caring at the beginning of a relationship. The narcissist appears this way in order to be in good favor and gain appreciation. The codependent does this in efforts of lavishing attention on the other to start the dependency ball rolling. Whereas the codependent easily becomes prey to the charm of the narcissist, the narcissist quickly falls for the codependent's offers of complete control. The codependent will voluntarily sacrifice boundaries, personal goals and desires, even their own needs, in order to please the narcissist, who in turn, loves the role of the 'be-all' to the codependent. Sadly, this 'honeymoon' phase is really a trap, which is bound to end in misery. Once the codependent has conquered winning over the relationship status with the narcissist and vice versa, the codependent is now in the role of self-sacrifice, and the narcissist no longer needs their charm so overtly stated as in the beginning; the narcissist now believes they are entitled to the codependent. Regrettably, the craving for admiration, attention, and love craved by the codependent will most likely never appear again. The more the codependent desperately tries to revive those sentiments, the more attention is given to the narcissist and less is received by the codependent.

Narcissists are harmful to the codependent, as well as self-centered and controlling. The codependent who is self-sacrificing, giving and enveloped with the needs and wants of others, have blurred boundaries (a recurring theme in this book); the codependent does not know how to disconnect emotionally with the narcissist. Like a bad habit, codependents repeatedly show up on the dysfunctional dance floor attracted to partners who counter-match perfectly to their submissive, acquiescent style of dance. The codependent finds this particular type of partner, to dysfunctionally dance with, very appealing. They are continuously attracted to the dominance, confidence, and charm so easily displayed by the narcissist. When the two pair up, the dance experience can boom with excitement...at least at the start. After many go-'rounds, the 'thrill of the dance', as expected, transforms into major conflict, drama, and entrapment. Even so, neither dare to put an end to it.

With the two paired up, the codependent/narcissist dance plays out flawlessly with the narcissist always maintaining the lead with the codependent following (always being careful not to step on the narcissist's toes). Their parts in the dance seem all too natural to the pair because they both have been practicing for it their whole lives. Seemingly instinctual, the codependent voluntarily gives up their power leaving the narcissist to thrive upon it. As usual, the narcissist receives much more than they give. The codependent is seemingly stuck dancing for song after song naïvely hoping for their partner to finally understand they have needs, too. With the heartbreak of unfulfilled hopes, the codependent quietly and bitterly swallows their misery. They are basically cemented in a pattern of sacrificing and giving with no chance of ever receiving the same from the other. While pretending to enjoy the dance, they are really harboring feelings of bitterness and sorrow for not ever leading the dance. They feel as if they know for a fact that they will never find another caring dance partner. They have developed a form of learned helplessness due to their low self-worth and pessimism, which ends up keeping them in the dysfunctional dance with the narcissist. Although the codependent wishes for balance and harmony, they sabotage themselves consistently by choosing relationships with individuals to whom they are attracted initially, but in the end will resent. Without self-worth or feelings of independence, the codependent is not able to choose a partner capable of mutual respect. The fear of abandonment and feelings of powerlessness is an extension of their youth where they yearned to be respected, cared for and loved.

As for the codependent, there is no end in sight to this relationship due to the fact that they will deem it as a personal failure. Remember it is the "job" of the codependent to rescue the relationship. The narcissist will 'stick around' as long as they keep being the center of attention and getting their needs met...but, just providing slight encouragement enough to keep the spark of hope alive in the codependent. The narcissist doesn't feel responsible for any wrongdoings due to their lack of empathy, so there is no reason for them to change. This leaves the couple's relationship ending in the hands of the codependent. However, due to fear of being alone and a lack of self-worth, the codependent feels they are better off trapped in a loveless and one-sided relationship. Usually, the relationship does not come to an end until the codependent has reached a breaking point, and even then, are highly unlikely to seek professional help or join a support group.

4

THE STAGES OF CODEPENDENCY

For romantic relationships and friendships, these stages are more easily observed and identified than in family relationships, as later discussed. In the early stage, the codependent starts to become increasingly involved in an unhealthy obsession with someone. Dysfunctional behavior is rationalized or denied. They start to give up their own hobbies, friends and interests. In the middle stage, self-blame, guilt, and anxiety play a bigger role in the relationship and when receiving nothing in return, disappointment and resentment start to grow. The codependent may start being dishonest, manipulative, blaming and nagging in attempts to change the other person with whom they are involved. A strong potential arises for harmful eating, dieting, compulsive gambling, or shopping, and excessive use of drugs and alcohol. The codependent may try changing their loved one by nagging or manipulating them. They may be dishonest about their partner's behavior to family and friends. The late stage of codependency begins to affect the individual physically and mentally. Often, disorders related to stress, such as headaches, stomach problems, insomnia, sciatica, muscle fatigue, and heart disease, can arise. If addiction is happening, it will worsen. The codependent's self-worth hits rock bottom, hopelessness sets in, and the individual stops caring for themselves. At this point, the codependent urgently needs help.

The following describes the stages of codependency:

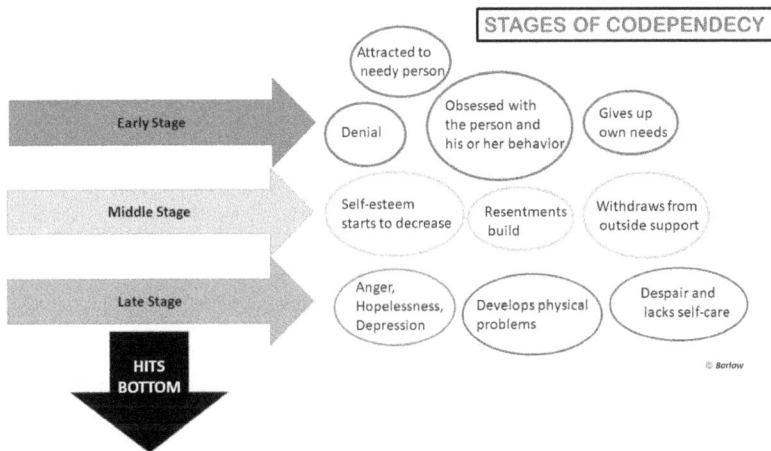

STAGES OF CODEPENDECY

Early Stage — Attracted to needy person / Denial / Obsessed with the person and his or her behavior / Gives up own needs

Middle Stage — Self-esteem starts to decrease / Resentments build / Withdraws from outside support

Late Stage — Anger, Hopelessness, Depression / Develops physical problems / Despair and lacks self-care

HITS BOTTOM

© Barlow

Early Stage

- Looks like a normal relationship, with increased attention and dependency on a partner and a strong need to please.
- Codependents may find themselves attracted to needy people, or be overly involved in a friend's life and wanting to help them, offering help, gifts and meals.
- Over time, the codependent becomes increasingly dependent on them for emotional validation and begins to give up

independent hobbies and activities in order to focus more on the other person and with them.

- Attempts to please the person.
- Obsessed with other's behaviors.
- Rationalizes and doubts own perceptions.
- Denial about codependency, but concern grows.
- Family and social life are affected.

Middle Stage

- Increased effort to minimize painful aspects of the relationship.
- The codependent may start covering for a partner with substance abuse to minimize the extent of the problem.
- Hides painful aspects of relationships from others.
- Anxiety, guilt, and self-blame increase.
- Self-esteem lessens.
- Tries to control by nagging, blaming, and manipulation.
- Feels resentment at inability to control the person.
- Enables and manages the person's responsibilities.
- Withdraws from outside family and friends.

Late Stage

- Develops physical symptoms.
- Digestive and sleep problems.
- Headaches, muscle tension, or pain.
- Eating disorders and Temporomandibular Joint Disorders

(TMJ).

- Obsessive-compulsive behavior or other addictions increase.
- Feels angry, hopeless, and depressed.
- Despair and lack of self-care.
- Increased conflicts.
- Further decline in self-esteem.

CODEPENDENCY, CHILDHOOD TRAUMA AND POST-TRAUMATIC STRESS DISORDER

In the context of family members, the development of codependency often happens so early that they aren't easily broken down into stages. Trauma is injurious in many ways, from psychological, to emotional, to physical and relational. Any kind of trauma can lead to codependent relationships. These relationships can develop in a family system or an intimate relationship. Unfortunately, too many individuals suffer from childhood trauma, and not enough of them were provided with the resources to cope with it. Experiencing trauma as a child is one of the main causes behind codependency. A strong reason is that childhood trauma is usually family-centered neglect, abuse, substance abuse, verbal and emotional abuse or constant arguing. This often results in an adult who is very helpless or an adult who needs to be needed. A review of the literature revealed that traumatic childhood experiences, have a long-lasting impact on individuals, including:

- Chronic physical illness;
- Bipolar Disorder;
- Borderline Personality Disorder;

- Depression;
- Chemical Dependency;
- Suicidal ideations and/or attempts; and
- Post-Traumatic Stress Disorder (PTSD).

Sometimes something can be noticed that has only a vague reminder of a past situation that was traumatic and can trigger the mind's readiness for a freeze, fight-or-flight response. Examples include: a triggered flight response to perceiving a threat, causing an intense need to flee; a freeze response takes over in the form of dissociation, numbing-out, or oversleeping; a fight response happens when the response is one of aggression fueled with adrenaline. Many individuals suffering from trauma develop an ability over time to use a combination of these responses based on the nature of the circumstances.

Another triggered reaction seen in the codependent, that stems from childhood trauma, is learning how to relinquish the fight response. This means no backtalk, due to a lack of the development of assertive language skills. The child has also learned from an early age that they cannot outrun a parent and hopelessly must stay in the harmful atmosphere. Therefore, the child must bypass the defense mechanism of the fight response, causing them to slip further into the freeze response, slowly drifting into a dissociative state, which can later develop into an addiction to numbing substances, such as marijuana, alcohol, and opiate, or other sedative-type drugs. Finally, the child learns, after realizing they cannot run, hide, or fight their way out of the trauma, that they may be safer if they are helpful, useful or needed, leading them into a life-long struggle of servitude. All boundaries are surrendered, and the child has become a parentified housekeeper, friend, parent to other siblings, and sounding board and landing in adult life as a codependent destined to repeat the cycle if they do not seek help. This all starts before the child has any insight and develops into immediately becoming servile when there is any hint of danger.

It is awful to think of a human being behaving like an animal that remains loyal to an abusive master out of fear of being harmed. Clarification of this concept is necessary but not enough for recovery. Some codependents understand their habit of giving up on themselves, but seem to, without consideration, forget everything they have learned about appropriate differentiation in their relationships. To break free from subservience, the codependent has to have the cognitive insight to identify the fear that triggers the aforementioned responses to trauma and practice increasing their skills of responses, which are more functional.

One possible result of experiencing trauma is dysfunctional relationships. Even when only one individual in the pair has experienced trauma, it has a ripple effect for all of the people close to that person. Significant others can experience secondary effects from the trauma, or feel traumatized by witnessing their loved one's reaction to trauma. Forming healthy relationships and bonding with others is one of the most challenging parts of life. When traumatized, a person can form loyalty to others in an unhealthy way, which is called 'trauma-bonding'. This means that the traumatized individual has a tendency of having abnormal attachments to another when in the presence of exploitation, danger, or shame. There is a tendency for more abuse, dishonesty, obsession, and self-sabotage when entering into this type of relationship. Another unfortunate aspect of codependency is resulting from another's addiction. In this relationship, the codependent offers a type of dysfunctional helping where they enable or support another person's abuse of substances, irresponsibility, defective mental health or under-achievement. Healthy relationships, which are supportive in nature, are essential for a person recovering from trauma. However, too frequently codependency is the result of complex trauma and childhood trauma.

5

LOOKING FOR A LIFELINE

The importance of getting help cannot be underestimated when it comes to codependents. Each treatment protocol is unique to each client. These symptoms are completely reversible with help from a professional and the assistance of support groups. A specialist in the field of codependency can help you recognize and verbalize your concerned feelings, thoughts and actions. If there are secondary psychological issues, such as depression, anxiety, and/or PTSD, medication may be considered alongside therapy. It is possible to regain your own identity, improve your self-esteem and gain ownership over your needs, thoughts, feelings and desires. By working with a therapist and attending support meetings, you will learn how to stop enabling behaviors, set appropriate boundaries, and reform healthy relationships with those you love. Eventually, your happiness will depend on you. Your life will include things that interest you, attainable goals, and the innovative energy with which to pursue them.

Codependents do not usually get help for themselves until they 'hit bottom' or there is a big enough crisis, or they are suffering to the breaking point. Sometimes, they are not even aware, or they are in denial about the abuse or their significant other's addiction. Recovery starts with breaking through that denial and becoming educated about the reasons behind the condition. Learning through reading the literature is a good start, but the real change happens when you seek therapy and attend Twelve-Step programs (later explained in this chapter), such as Al-Anon and CoDA. Codependency doesn't just stop automatically when an individual leaves a dysfunctional relationship. Recovery requires ongoing support and maintenance. After years of recovery, the codependent's thinking and actions start to internalize, and the skills learned lead to new and healthy habits. Even so, codependency can return quite easily if you enter into another dysfunctional relationship; relapse happens without due diligence. There is no such thing as a perfect recovery. Slipping back into old behaviors simply offers a new learning experience! With recovery, hope is renewed, and focus is shifted back onto yourself. There are three stages of recovery:

THE EARLY STAGE OF RECOVERY: PRECONTEMPLATION

In the early stage of recovery from codependency, the denial starts to break down. You are ready to face reality and confront the issue that is necessary in order to change it. This early stage may be encouraged by another person in recovery or a close friend that knows of your suffering. This is a real wake-up call, also known as hitting bottom. Change becomes of the utmost importance and instead of minimizing the issues, you decide to face them, even with them being as difficult and painful as they are. Starting recovery begins by obtaining information and asking for help.

As the codependency gets worse in severity, as do the consequences. During the early stages of recovery, the codependent has had to come to terms with their reality that life has become unmanageable, that they have been in denial and minimizing the dysfunction in the relationship. The person may even know at this point that they are codependent. However, a person in the early stage of recovery still wants to remain in the chaos rather than try and change their circumstances. Briefly, the perceived comfort of continuing to remain in the relationship is thought to be better than the consequences.

* * *

See the following table for the comparison of the stages of codependency versus the stages of recovery.

Progression of Codependency	Recovery from Codependency
Finds themselves attracted to a dysfunctional relationship.	Hits bottom and asks for help.
People-pleasing.	Educates themselves about codependency.
Obsessions about the significant other.	Starts therapy and/or Twelve-Step Meetings.
Doubts and rationalizes their own perceptions.	Begins to feel hope.
Denial about the other's addiction, abuse, and other dysfunctional characteristics.	Breaks through denial.
Gives up their own friends and activities and becomes engulfed by the other's needs, wants, and desires.	Learns that recovery is a selfish program.
Family life is negatively affected.	Starts to focus on themselves.
Falls deeper into dysfunction and codependency.	Begins to build their own identity.

THE MIDDLE STAGE OF RECOVERY: CONTEMPLATION

Transitioning from the early stage to the middle stage is one of contemplation. This stage is considered when the consequences of the relationship are much worse than they had thought. In fact, the codependent is starting to be very aware of the bad effects that the relationship is doing to them, however, they are not quite positive that the bad effects outweigh the codependent's habitual comfort of staying in the abuse. It is during this stage that the codependent starts to open up to the idea of recovery; while they have not actually thoroughly decided to get help, the person has started to feel that recovery has to be inevitable at some time in the future.

They may even openly start to verbalize they have a problem. However, if any attempts are made to push the codependent into getting help, they will usually have some type of excuse as to why they have to put it off until sometime in the future. Sometimes, it may even seem like a valid excuse.

During the middle stage, the codependent also begins to learn about building their self-esteem, own boundaries, identity, and how to express their feelings with a healthy assertiveness.

At this point, the codependent starts to move in the direction of preparation; they realize that the consequences of staying in the dysfunctional relationship are far worse than any benefits they can think of. With addiction, they come to the conclusion that changes in behavior are necessary for their health.

Now, there is an acknowledgement that help is needed. Hence, thus beginning the preparation stage. Once here, the codependent realizes that getting help will be life changing. It is also at this time that the codependent begins to become proactive by educating themselves and starts to search for different available resources.

The Middle Stage of Recovery: Action

During the action stage, the codependent dives into recovery by seeing a professional, joining a Twelve-Step group, and using various other tools available, such as codependency workbooks and life coaching. But the action stage is more than just getting help, rather the codependent makes a commitment to change their lifestyle, one which will provide a healthier, happier and more productive future. During the action stage, the codependent is also looking for other ways to enhance their new lifestyle, such as exercise, nutritional plans, and career goals, along with re-establishing relationships on a healthier foundation.

Independence, mental hygiene, spiritual fitness, and self-dialog are all important aspects of recovery from codependency and are also heavily influenced by physical condition. Most people realize that exercise is good for their body, however, it is the relationship to their mental state that is underestimated. Our ancestors instinctually hunted and gathered, continually expending energy to meet their needs. The human body is clearly designed for that type of energy expenditure. Plus, exercise releases the brain's natural endorphins, such as adrenaline, serotonin, and other inherent antidepressants. Rather than taking a pill to feel better (unless prescribed by your doctor), take a nature walk if you are feeling down. The best way to keep exercising is to make it a habit or part of your daily routine. Keep it up, along with positive affirmations and soon you will notice a big difference in how you feel. Showing up is what counts, worry about how long and how much later. Most of all try and make it an enjoyable event so that you will look forward to it as rewarding.

THE LATE STAGE OF RECOVERY: MAINTENANCE

Now that the codependent has passed the early and middle stages, which included precontemplation, contemplation and action, they must now take on the responsibility of maintaining their newly acquired independence. This stage is of great importance, because if not taken to heart, it can lead to relapse. Fortunately, there are many resources available for this stage of recovery: CoDA, Al-Anon,

Alumni groups, therapy, aftercare, religious affiliations, and other support groups. Much like needing to practice a new skill, the codependent in this stage must practice maintenance. In the late stage, self-worth and happiness no longer depend on someone else. What is gained is the capacity for both independence and intimacy. The codependent will experience their own sense of power and self-love. They will experience an expansive, uninhibited innovativeness, with the ability to produce and pursue their own goals.

What is a Twelve-Step Recovery Program and Does It Work?

Codependents Anonymous (CA), Narcotics Anonymous (NA), and Alcoholics Anonymous (AA) are among mutual self-help groups, which operate under the guidelines of twelve steps and twelve traditions. The twelve steps encourage honesty, faith, and self-probing humility. These groups are led by peers, are free of charge, and meet on a regular basis. These twelve faith-based steps were to be followed by recovering alcoholics. The basic premise is a step-by-step guideline that introduces practices meant to create more self-awareness and a willingness to accept help. These practices also focus on consciously changing thought and behavior patterns, and maintaining recovery once achieved.

Most interestingly, when AA was founded in 1936, many were unsure and cynical that those addicts could find recovery based on a set of spiritually based principles. Doctor prescriptions? Sure. Behavioral therapy? Of course. But relying on a higher power for recovery? At the time, many psychology experts believed that alcoholics could in no way be helped by a support group that was as 'touchy-feely' as AA. However, to the surprise of all, AA and other twelve-step groups soared with ever-increasing popularity. As of today, there are in excess of 2 million AA members with 115,000 AA groups, and that is not counting NA, CA, Coda, Gamblers Anonymous (GA), and many others. There are literally thousands of meetings for every morning, day and evening in every location. Often, the group halls are open 24 hours during holidays. They produce social events, such as Christmas parties, Valentine's dances, barbecues, and other chemical or misbehaved free get-togethers. AA believes that there is no cure for alcoholism, and remaining sober requires perpetual self-awareness and effort. These programs are based on community, bringing together people from all walks of life who share a common struggle. Listening to success stories from others makes recovery feel achievable. Sharing setbacks and failures reduces the feeling that you are 'unfixable'.

A review of research indicated the main factor of change is the primary aspect of mutual-help groups. The studies reviewed concluded that by even adding one friend in recovery to your social circle increases your chances of staying clean by 25%. In addition to meeting other people who are struggling with the same issues as they are, codependents can contact other members and get a sponsor whenever they need inspirational support, which is much like group therapy on an informal level. This is one of the many reasons CoDA and Al-Anon are so effective. After reviewing the literature, it is quite obvious that dismissing Twelve-Step programs as unscientific because they are faith-based is inconsistent with the large body of in-depth research acquired throughout the past 25 years.

WHAT ARE THE TWELVE STEPS?

Through meetings in a group with others who are in the program, an individual who joins a Twelve-step group usually gets a sponsor who works together with the codependent and guides them through the **Twelve Steps**. These include:

1. We admitted we were powerless over others, that our lives had become unmanageable.
2. Came to believe that a power greater than ourselves could restore us to sanity.
3. Made a decision to turn our will and lives over to the care of God, as we understood God.
4. Made a searching and fearless moral inventory of ourselves.
5. Admitted to God, to ourselves, and to another human being, the exact nature of our wrongs.
6. Were entirely ready to have God remove all these defects of character.
7. Humbly asked God to remove our shortcomings.
8. Made a list of all persons we had harmed and became willing to make amends to them all.
9. Made direct amends to such people wherever possible, except when to do so would injure them or others.
10. Continued to take personal inventory and, when we were wrong, promptly admitted it.
11. Sought through prayer and meditation to improve our conscious contact with God as we understood God, praying

only for knowledge of God's will for us and the power to carry that out (CoDa.org).

12. Having had a spiritual awakening as the result of these steps, we tried to carry this message to other codependents and to practice these principles in all our affairs.

The Twelve CoDA Traditions:

1. Our common welfare should come first; personal recovery depends upon CoDA unity.

2. For our group purpose, there is but one ultimate authority, a loving higher power as expressed to our group conscience. Our leaders are but trusted servants; they do not govern.

3. The only requirement for membership in CoDA is a desire for healthy and loving relationships.

4. Each group should remain autonomous except in matters affecting other groups or CoDA as a whole.

5. Each group has but one primary purpose: to carry its message to other codependents who still suffer.

6. A CoDA group ought never endorse, finance, or lend the CoDA name to any related facility or outside enterprise, lest problems of money, property and prestige divert us from our primary spiritual aim.

7. A CoDA group ought to be fully self-supporting, declining outside contributions.

8. CoDependents Anonymous should remain forever nonprofessional, but our service centers may employ special workers.

9. CoDA, as such, ought never be organized, but we may create service boards or committees directly responsible to those they serve.

10. CoDA has no opinion on outside issues; hence, the CoDA name ought never be drawn into public controversy.

11. Our public relations policy is based on attraction rather than promotion; we need to always maintain personal anonymity at the level of press, radio, and films.

12. Anonymity is the spiritual foundation of all our traditions; ever reminding us to place principles before personalities.

Twelve Promises for a fulfilled life: People pledge to engage in the following twelve promises while recovering:

1. I have a new sense of belonging, and any feelings of emptiness or loneliness will eventually fade away.

2. I am no longer controlled by my fears, and instead I overcome them to "act with courage, integrity and dignity".

3. I know a freedom from codependency and unhealthy dynamics.

4. I release feelings of shame and guilt, as well as regrets about the past. I cannot change what has happened, but I can act so it doesn't happen again.

5. I feel genuinely lovable, loving and loved. I accept myself and others as we are.

6. I see myself as an equal in current and future relationships.

7. I maintain healthy and loving relationships, without needing

to control what those people do. I learn to trust those around me.

8. I recognize it is possible to heal and change while maintaining healthy boundaries with my family.
9. I recognize I am "a unique and precious creation". No one in the world can be me, besides me.
10. I know my own worth without needing the validation of others.
11. I trust myself innately and believe that I am able to guide myself.
12. I experience more serenity, strength, and spiritual growth each day.

Exercise

1. Write down a list of the things your loved one does that trigger these feelings of failure so that you can reflect upon them during your recovery journey.
2. Sort these things into 3 categories
3. Things I can control;
4. Things they can control; and
5. Things neither of us can control.

Possible actions for Change

- Limiting contact: removes opportunities for you to ask questions or offer unsolicited advice.
- Set physical boundaries. Decide how much energy and time

you want to give to each individual in your life. If someone is toxic, set firm boundaries about the length of time you will spend together.

- Establish emotional boundaries. If you cannot limit your time spent with a toxic individual, set limits on how much emotional energy you are willing to spend on them. In your spare time, do not spend it complaining about them. Remember, you can regulate how *you* feel. Your day does not depend on what side of the bed a toxic person gets up on!

- At first, you may feel as if you are abandoning that person, but in order for them to live a fulfilled life they have to be able to make decisions for themselves.

- Reduce friction between you and your loved one.

- Work on self-control not on controlling others. Set your focus on how you react to others—assert yourself or walk away—it is *your* choice.

- Follow through with what you say or plan. Repeated warnings or threats to stop lending money—just to do it again—makes matters worse. Be a person of your word, or you will be adding to the relationship's dysfunction.

- Regulate your thinking. If you catch yourself having destructive thoughts, create a healthy self-dialog, reminding you of your decisions and telling yourself you are no longer a victim.

- Practice healthy coping skills. People can and will still be draining on your emotions, even when you have set good boundaries. It is imperative that you practice strategies that will help you cope and stay strong.

- Use various coping skills, such as mediation and writing a gratitude list.
- Tend to your health.
- Stay true to your set of values by prioritizing them.
- Build your mental muscles. If you do not exercise your mental muscles, they will atrophy just like physical muscles. Give up negative habits that are draining your mental strength. The stronger you become, the less draining are toxic people, giving them less power over you; they are then less likely to take a toll on your health.
- Use your support system. Rally your support network. It will feel so much better to vent to someone who values you.
- Let yourself be strengthened by your motives. Control your decision-making power, rather than letting it be controlled by someone else. Personal power has nothing to do with what someone else thinks, it has everything to do with your beliefs, that you will not be a victim.
- It is important to understand that takers usually see in other people what they do not want to see in themselves (projection). You can be the most generous, kind, and nicest person in the world and the taker will nearly 'kill' themselves trying to turn you into a monster. Understand why they're seeing what they see in you.

Have you ever noticed that, when something isn't working for us, we have a tendency to do the same thing more before we try another way? The same goes for the codependent; things may get worse before the taker stops the abuse. They will try every manipulation known to mankind to try and control you. Take their increase in tyranny as a sign that their old ways will no longer work, and they will move onto the next victim. Keep up the good work so they know you are sticking to your guns. Teach those with an unhealthy dependency on you that you are not responsible for their habitual crises and that you will not partake in their pity party anymore. Do offer to help or ask a lot of questions; you are not dealing with a normal individual. Toxic individuals will tear down your boundaries before you even realize you have them built. Know just what you will take and what you won't, and how far you are willing to let someone intrude on your boundaries; listen to that practiced self-dialog, "It just isn't worth it anymore".

You are still a compassionate, understanding, respectful and kind human being, but be all of that to yourself first. Compassion exists wonderfully with strength. You can dismiss certain behaviors, people and their requests, without becoming someone you don't like. It will be empowering to feel OK about your boundaries as long as you haven't hurt another in the process. Remember, sometimes helping is hurting. Own your weaknesses as well as your strengths; everyone is a work in progress. Know that your weaknesses cannot be used against you; that is how the taker tries to gain power. They will work tirelessly to play down your strengths while amping up your weaknesses. Once you are aware of your flaws, nobody can use them against you. There is no reasoning with a toxic person. Make your stance and stand strong. You are handling a person whose motivation is controlling and taking advantage of what is not good for either of you. Try not to focus on anger and resentment; focus on the solution. If you know or think you are about to make a poor decision, focus on the consequences, not on the person who is trying to ruin your life.

Surround yourself with like people; those who give the way you do. You may not be able to actually decide on how much freedom you have in specific parts of your life, but you can choose who is in it and who is not. Then you can choose, from those who are in, to which ones you want to open up your heart. You know you have no control over the past, but you can control how much you let it affect the present and to what extent it will impact your future. Forgiveness is about letting go of thinking things will be different. Self-love is necessary for forgiveness, because it is accomplished with strength. However, don't forget the way you have been treated and use those memories to add clarity to your life. Remember the codependency patterns of fear and the patterns of the taker. At first, they charm, then provide attention, love, and affection. Next, they gain your trust, and then they drain you of all that you are. Be aware of the cycle, so it doesn't repeat itself.

MAKING AMENDS

An important part of recovery is taking action toward making amends. It is essential to your mental health. Think of it as something you are doing for yourself, not just the person to whom you are making amends. Each time you conquer uncomfortable circumstances, you grow spiritually. Taking that step of owning your mistakes, makes it much easier to progress forward. Everyone involved in a previous mistake benefits when amends are made. Thinking that you are that one person in the whole world who doesn't owe anyone an apology has you standing a good chance there are some resentments looming around in your life. Own your mistakes, make amends, and then put it behind you; it's cleansing. This is an action-based step in your recovery process. The circumstance was difficult enough and now it has had time to brew into potential resentment. Ignoring it does not make it go away. The person who feels upset or injured will harbor those feelings as they grow stronger with each day that passes without resolution.

It can be terribly uncomfortable, and if you have been going back and forth in your mind as to whether or not to make amends, chances are it is time to do so. Fearing anger in the other and allowing procrastination to take over associates with negativity in your mind. Facing the fear builds your character in a strong and healthy direction. Just know that you have probably associated mistakes with being a bad person, or that saying you're sorry is a sign of weakness. This is part of the shame-based developmental aspects of being codependent. In actuality, it is just the opposite; making amends is a sign of great strength and fearlessness and that you are moving in a positive direction.

SELF-DOUBT

Self-doubt is connected to self-dialog in a negative manner. It also becomes like a bad habit. Individuals who can become comfortable with self-doubt can become, in essence, lazy. Why bother trying something if you are already convinced it can't be accomplished. To remedy the problem of self-doubt, it first has to be acknowledged. It takes perseverance and inner-strength. You have to hold yourself accountable for not putting a stronger effort into your endeavors. Some individuals believe only in dreams of new jobs or moving across the sea, but, then there are those who realize their dreams without doubting their abilities to make them come true. Participate fully in your life, and do your best to not be on the sidelines of envy wishing you never doubted yourself.

Trying your best means not trying to be perfect; that only increases self-doubt because perfection is rarely attainable. Do you know many happy perfectionists? Also, if you are regularly comparing yourself to someone else, it will be nearly impossible to cure self-doubt. Why tell yourself you are unsuccessful in life because you do not have that big pool that your neighbor has? But still, try to strive for the pool that you want in your backyard and make it a reality. Having compassion for yourself will be rewarded with positivity and will interrupt self-criticism. If you bump into a case of self-doubt, examine the truth behind it, and ask yourself, "What is the worst that can happen?" Self-doubt is grounded in unfounded predictions of fear and failure. Before you hit the road, take a look at a map. Then, you will not doubt your path.

FEELING OVERWHELMED

These days, most people are very busy and, therefore, it is easy to feel overwhelmed, making it difficult to keep things in the right perspective. The key to coping during these stressful times is to take 'baby steps' and to take your time. Feeling overwhelmed can be all-consuming, draining you of your energy and distorting your reality. Left unattended to, it will also lead you to burning out or 'freaking out'. It can also be a bit tricky to identify because the way it looks and the way it feels come in various forms. At times, feeling overwhelmed may seem like it is 'all too much', and you do not know what to do next. It can come in the form of fatigue, impatience, irritability, and lack of focus. This often happens when the codependent is trying to meet everyone else's expectations, and there is not enough time spent on themselves. When it happens, life seems like one big struggle and feels like you are barely treading water with 1,000 pounds strapped to your back. Thinking can come negatively in black and white when feeling this way: "I am the worst partner, mother, employee, friend, etc.!" Every person is going to be overwhelmed at some point in time, and yet when in the midst of it, you can feel like you are completely alone. The codependent will keep telling themselves, "I should be able to handle this." This only adds fuel to the fire and makes them feel even worse.

Codependents have come to believe that they must be helpful and selfless and that other people's needs are much more important than their own, thinking they have to be amenable, obliging, 'good' people. This conditioning from early childhood has taught the codependent the false belief that they should be able to do everything known to man, to please everyone at all times, and to do it with a smile on their face. And so, if they cannot, because, of course, it is not possible, they become overwhelmed and feel like a failure. Reliable and responsible are 'must-dos' for people who are codependent, thinking if they disappoint anyone, they are a bad person. If you are in a relationship as a partner or parent or family member, and you're trying to be perfect—handling other people's stress—all the while comparing yourself to them, and then beating yourself up because you don't think you're good enough, your identity and happiness will surely fade.

The question is what do you do? The first thing to do when trying to reduce your feelings of being overwhelmed is to question yourself about what is important right this second. Not what you or someone else should or wants you to do, but what are *your* needs in this moment. Maybe it is time to take a few deep breaths in your nose and out of your mouth or have a cool glass of water; try going for a walk, meditating, or any of the stress-reducing techniques mentioned in this book. Next, question yourself about the basics, such as sleep/rest, food, and water, or have you been gassing up with sugar and caffeine? Then, decide on one baby step you can take to rebalance yourself, even if it is in just one aspect, and 'just do it'. If you do not meet your basic needs, coping can be a real problem. When feeling over-whelmed, your mind cannot cope with the demands of your emotions and body, so commit yourself to taking a baby step to move you out of being overwhelmed.

By taking action and actually participating in a stress-management plan, you are taking back control of your life so that the problem of feeling chronically overwhelmed no longer rules your life. Then you will be able to figure out specifically what is making you feel over-whelmed and institute the steps necessary for reducing it. By acknowl-edging that you have too much on your shoulders, because you believe you have to say "yes" to every request, you can start the process of sticking to your boundaries by firmly and politely, saying "no". You do not need to give a long-winded explanation to anyone as to why something is too much; it doesn't make you a weak, selfish, or bad person. It simply means that you have a finite amount of energy and time. As discussed later in the book, asking for help is an indication of inner-strength, not a weakness. Trying to conquer feeling overwhelmed on your own is, itself, overwhelming! So, start by recognizing when the feeling starts, asking for help, and naming the baby steps that you will take to guide you gently back into a state of peace and calmness.

SELF-IMPROVEMENT

Everyone talks about improving themselves in one way or another. Rather than setting unrealistic goals, try a few of these simple steps; all you need is willingness, consistency, and determination, and the quality of your life can change for the better.

1. Have the willingness to work hard, and this means for you not for others. Like everything else in life, if you want success in anything, you have to put the work in to get it. This doesn't mean to exhaust yourself leaving you feeling down in the dumps.

2. Make sure you have a healthy support system. Sharing the load by communicating and taking feedback on how you are doing helps and is important for self-improvement. We can all use encouragement to keep us going during tough times. It is important to have people around us whom we respect enough that we would listen when they tell us how it is even when you don't want to hear it.

3. Do not overthink your situation, adapt to it. People hit difficult periods in life, such as the loss of a job or divorce. Rather than overanalyzing the problem, accept and adapt to your circumstances. Briefly

ask yourself if spending a vast amount of time analyzing a situation in any way can change it; if the answer is no, do not waste anymore of your emotions trying to change something with an outcome that you are powerless to attain.

4. Effective time management is very important. We have only a short time on this planet, so use it wisely. Take a look at your day; is it a daily grind? It is most likely time to try something new and to make it something you enjoy. Evaluate how much time you waste on worrying, obsessional thinking about another person's behavior, ruminating about rescuing, etc.

5. Stay consistent with your improvements. If you have decided to take a 15-minute walk each day, don't quit after three walks. Stick to your commitment. Can you imagine how many people pay good money to join a gym and only go to it for the first few weeks after having paid for a year's membership?

6. Locate your happy place where you find serenity and contentment, as long as it is a healthy place. Try meditation and, with your eyes closed, develop a beautiful happy place to go to in your mind that you can go back and visit regularly.

7. Embrace each emotion, even the difficult ones. Sometimes your emotions can bring out your joy and sometimes your fears. Embrace each one, as they come up in your life, wholeheartedly so you can understand them and then let them go. Do your best not to resist them because 'what you resist, persists'.

8. Always be ready to step outside of your comfort zone. The concept of stepping outside of your comfort zone can be a paralyzing fear for

some, however, it is necessary for any major change. You don't have to go skydiving. However, it is not a bad idea to try something you once feared, like doing something alone just for you. It doesn't have to be way out of your comfort zone, but it does need to be a challenge for you.

9. Stay present and live in the here and now. It is within this moment that gratitude can be felt for all that you appreciate and in the beauty of the simple things in life. Being mindful of what is happening in your life right now and taking yourself to where you belong will bring about a better quality of life instead of the incessant worry and stress about your past or your future (both do not exist right now).

10. Try learning something new. Learning new things makes your world much bigger and can build your self-confidence and self-esteem. Going to a Twelve-Step group and meeting new people will have you feeling on top of your game and wanting to share your experience, strength, and hope with others that they may find peace and happiness, too.

The following are helpful exercises for identifying and working through potential codependency traits:

11. Write down the symptoms you have learned, and you relate to. Not all will be relevant. Identifying the symptoms most apparent in your life makes it easier to look for solutions tailored to your experiences.

- Optional follow-up: Family history exercise.
- Look at the list of symptoms and identify any that you

remember observing in family members, especially when you were younger. Understanding why your family/parents acted in a certain way makes it easier to unlearn that inherited behavior.

12. Practice self-care.

- An important component to breaking the cycle of codependency is realizing you are complete on your own. By practicing nourishing and caring for yourself, you will gain a sense of empowerment.
- Techniques for self-care can include: meditation, breathing exercises, taking a class, going to the gym, nature walks, and other solo exercises will improve your self-worth, along with your mental and physical health.

13. Develop decision-making skills.

- Take note of instances when you are depending on another person when trying to make a decision.
- Try going with your gut and inner self when determining your best choices.

14. Cultivate independence.

- Do things by yourself that you usually want to do with someone else in order to feel comfortable. Try hiking, going out to eat or going to the movies alone. When you learn you can enjoy things on your own, you will discover a new relationship with yourself.

15. Consider therapy for past trauma.

- People do not need some drastic reason for seeing a counselor. There comes a time when every codependent notices the relationship they're in is not meeting their needs.
- A therapist can assist you in working through traumas from your relationships and childhood that are possibly causing you to act in codependent ways, as well as helping you define relationship patterns and establishing boundaries moving forward.

16. Exercise for resolving obsessional behaviors. (Note: If you've been sexually abused, this exercise should be conducted under the guidance of a professional.)

- Find a quiet and safe place where you can sit uninterrupted.
- Meditate on your true inner feelings, including fear, anger and sorrow.
- Think of a time when you were growing up that you felt the same way.
- What age were you?
- Who was the person or people responsible for these feelings? Were you told to stop crying or acting like a baby, or were you told you are overly sensitive?

- Were you made to feel shame, thereby making you repress your feelings?
- Next, tap into the emotions instead of repressing them and allow yourself to honestly really feel them. Anger may surface and tears may fall, but it is imperative that you move through the feelings until they are spent.

17. Relationship inventory.

- Make a list of people in your life who are important (spouse, lover, colleagues, family members and friends).
- Think about each relationship for a couple of minutes.
- Note the individuals on your list whom you believe to be dysfunctional.
- How many suffer from addiction or any form of mental illness?
- Note unbalanced relationships where you do all of the giving.
- Put away your list for 48 hours, then;
- Pick the most stressful relationship.
- Write down a boundary to set.
- Practice how to tell that significant person about the boundary with someone in your support system whom you trust (knowing they may not like it). I suggest that you put your list away for at least 24 hours. (This is a significant first step in your recovery from codependency.).

18. Stress-reducing relaxation.

- The path to conquering codependency lies in being able to relax and start a loving relationship with yourself.
- Be seated in a relaxed position and shut your eyes.
- Relax each muscle in your body starting with your toes and moving toward your face.
- Breathe through your nose and silently count 1 and then breathe out of your mouth slowly and count 1 and repeat. Do not try to control your breathing.
- Do this exercise every day for 10 minutes.

19. How to start focusing on yourself.

- When with someone else, remind yourself not to keep watch on the other person.
- Imagine putting that person's wants and needs in the hands of a higher power.
- Mindfully practice being non-judgmental.
- Write down your feelings in a journal.
- Take time-outs when starting to react to another's emotions and journal.
- Journal affirmations.

6

REWRITING YOUR LIFE STORY

"Whether we realize it or not, we all impose a narrative on our lives."

— JOAN DIDION

As you have come to understand from previous chapters, codependency is rooted in the belief that you are not good enough on your own. You feel unworthy when not serving others, and this lack of self-love allows you to give up healthy self-care routines in order to focus on other people. The extreme codependent feels empty inside, void of healthy feelings, and existing only for others. They do not exist as an individual and use other people like a drug or alcohol. The codependent feels that other people make them feel good and assist them in covering up their own feelings. The more they do for other people, the more highly they think of themselves. What story do you tell about yourself?

The beliefs most ingrained in our subconscious often form by the time we are 7 years old based on the behaviors we have observed around us. Attachment and bonding to caregivers are critical for survival, and we adapt our behaviors to work around the needs and actions of that caregiver. In unhealthy families, children receive acceptance and rewards from those around them, and they learn they have no power over how they feel. Since feelings and emotions are ignored in dysfunctional families, it is an unsafe environment in which to be vulnerable.

The conversations we have within ourselves mirror our experiences in life. Almost every step taken in life is simultaneously based on a memory. Our first experiences come from touching, smelling, tasting, and seeing, each of which triggers an emotion. The emotion then sparks a feeling that it labels as right, wrong, happy, or sad. Then, you apply a meaning to each of those experiences. Next, a meaning is registered to accompany each of those experiences. "I was adopted so my parents must have wanted to get rid of me." Or, "My parents adopted me because I am very special." Think of a time when you heard that voice inside of you saying, "be afraid". That voice has stopped you from many wonderful life experiences. This triggered anxiety is your mind's way of protecting you from repeating a mistake or a negative action. But it also reinforces that 'be afraid' story that you shouldn't do something. The good news is you get to choose your journey because you are the author. Your story doesn't only tell you why or how events happened in your life, it tells you which experiences were important. Either from a self-taught lesson or a spiritual awakening, the way you describe something to yourself is what makes it a memory.

You can begin the process of rewriting your life story by examining your interpretations of past experiences. Traumatic experiences can be repressed but still seriously influence your behaviors. One bad memory can have a snowball effect and create an anxiety disorder, triggering emotional terror. Everyone has bad memories, such as your first traffic ticket, first hangover, first trip to the dentist, etc. Once you learn how to rewrite your tale with an outcome that is full of resilience and heroic, you can achieve true peace. How you interpret events is up to you. It is possible to train your thought patterns to change the feelings associated with a memory to one with effective coping. If you have recalled a traumatic memory, start an inner dialog that tells you the lesson learned and how much stronger of a person it made you. Look back and revise your story to include how awesome, beautiful and intelligent you are. However, a traumatic memory is very different from a 'bad' memory and often needs an intervention on a professional level. Acceptance is the central component for coping with a traumatic memory. Your life story is a combination of your past reconstructed—how you perceive your present and how your future is imagined. All three exist together at the same time; they are linear and co-occurring, not separate. When you change the meaning and story of your past, your present and future are changed simultaneously and vice versa. Changing the meaning of your present and future story alters the meaning of your past at the same time.

Your story is constantly changing based on life experiences. No, you cannot change the facts of your past, but you can change the story you tell yourself. Your entire view of the world and your identity is a story with a meaning. Ask yourself: Is this story benefiting you? Is this the way you want to tell your story? Most likely, most of what you believe is based on the narrative you tell yourself; all of which are based on your past experiences. If you had trauma without any empathetic support to help your frame of mind can lead to dysfunction, fear, shame, guilt, and a whole gambit of unhealthy manifestations. You don't always have to have a plan for your day. Sometimes, it's best to let the day come to you...to let go of any obsessive thinking about how things should play out. When you are at peace with yourself, you can create what is around the next corner for yourself. You can pre-think your story and look for opportunities that are positive and healthy. There are those who seek comfortable atmospheres, and there are those who create comfortable atmospheres. You have to make the decision about which one you will seek.

Recovery means doing a 180-degree reversal of your dysfunctional patterns so that you can reconnect with your inner being, honor and self-care, and begin to behave from your core self. Healing from code-pendency redevelops your autonomy, authenticity, ability to be intimate, and integrated and harmonious thoughts, feelings, values, and behaviors. When it is time to edit your story, try not to distort reality, otherwise you may find it difficult accepting the best parts of you and accepting who you are. If you lie to yourself about yourself, you can have a rude awakening. Personal characteristics develop over the years into habits. Anything done repeatedly shapes into a habit, so mind your actions that had negative consequences. Poisonous narratives turn into low self-worth, self-doubt and self-pity. Spend time training yourself to notice distorted thinking. Some individuals believe they are the main topic of conversation and thought in everyone's lives. You have to address that distorted reality if it applies to you. Learning how to conquer irrational fears can be challenging. Anxiety and fear have much in common, however, they are not the same. Fear derives from perceived threats, while anxiety is a result of a fear that is anticipated.

Exercise: Challenging Limiting Beliefs

- **Step 1:** List beliefs you have about the world that inform how you act. Write this down in a journal or on a piece of paper (writing by hand makes more of a psychological impact).
- Ex: I am worth something when I am helping others.
- Ex: No family is truly happy.
- Ex: I can't be alone.
- **Step 2:** Recognize that these are things that FEEL true but are NOT. They are just beliefs. Write down where these beliefs may have come from (parents, siblings, home environment, teachers, etc.)
- **Step 3:** Come up with a belief that is aligned with what you want, rather than what you're working with right now. On that piece of paper, write a belief that challenges the ones you currently believe.
- Ex: I am worthy of space regardless of my actions.
- Ex: I can thrive independently of others.

You want to acknowledge this new belief and feel it. This won't be a process you do once and are finished with forever.

- **Step 4:** Take different actions.
- Act as if your new belief is true.
- Ex: How would you act if you truly felt you were worthy of space no matter what?
- You would most likely stand up for yourself, set boundaries, and be OK saying "No".
- Even small steps will help to undo the old belief and solidify this new, empowering thought.

Your old ways of dysfunctional coping, those entrenched in you, will keep tugging away, trying to send you into a panic. Once identified, you can calm the storm. Next are some breathing exercises that are proven to work by triggering the parasympathetic nervous system, which influences your body's ability to calm down and relax. The anxiety associated with our flight-or-fight response is ruled by the sympathetic nervous system. It is in the exhaling that works on anxiety.

Breathing Exercise 1: Lengthen your Exhale

If you take deep breaths too fast or too many of them, it can cause you to hyperventilate. When feeling anxiety and attempting to quell it by taking deep breaths too fast, we can increase the anxiety when we are actually trying to calm it.

1. This process can be done in any comfortable position.
2. Before taking a deep breath, fully exhale instead. Exhale all of the air out of your lungs, and then naturally inhale.
3. Inhale for 5 seconds
4. Exhale for 7 seconds
5. Do this for 3 minutes.

Breathing Exercise 2: Belly Breathing, Using your Diaphragm

1. Put one hand just above your belly button and the other hand in the middle of your chest.
2. While slowly breathing in with your nose, pay attention to your stomach rising.
3. Exhale through your mouth with pursed lips pushing all of the air out.
4. To make this breathing start to happen automatically, it takes daily practice for up to five minutes.

Breathing Exercise 3: Calming

1. Starting at your feet and moving up to your shoulders and face relax every muscle.
2. Take a slow deep breath while imagining the air coming in through the soles of your feet, traveling up your legs, through your stomach, and into your lungs, relaxing every muscle as the air passes through.
3. Slowly exhale, imagining the air leaving your lungs back into your belly, then your legs, and out of your feet.

4. Repeat until you are noticeably calm.

Breathing Exercise 4: Mindful Breathing

1. Put yourself in a comfortable position either sitting or laying down.
2. Slowly inhale through your nose, noticing your stomach expanding.
3. Slowly exhale through your mouth.
4. Repeat the pattern.
5. As your thoughts move into your head, notice there is no judgment, then release those thoughts and focus on your breathing.

WHAT IS SELF-CARE?

Did you know that 44% of people think self-care is possible only during leisure time? Many people associate self-care with 'treating yourself'—for example: getting a manicure, taking a bubble bath, or indulging in chocolate. These can be good practices to unwind after a long day, but don't actually target your mental or emotional health. People often just think about what will feel better in the moment and want to numb themselves instead of being proactive. True self-care is about taking actions that create a nurturing experience in the moment but also set you up for continued success. Many people believe it is selfish to make time for self-care. One coach proposes, "It's actually a selfish action not to engage in self-care because in order to care about the people in your lives, you have to care for yourself." With stillness comes a clearer picture and insight, and being active in your own care helps you to learn how to communicate, interact, and reach out. Mindfulness is by being emotionally present.

Self-care is deliberate actions needed to tend to our physical, mental and emotional health. Implementing self-care is essential to reducing anxiety and enhancing your mood. It is also important to the relationship you have with yourself and other people. It is not just knowing what self-care means; it is also what it doesn't mean. Self-care fuels you rather than drains you of your positive energy and well-being. It also is *not* selfish. It is knowing what needs to be done in order to take care of yourself and therefore to take care of others, too. By practicing self-care, you will learn how to cope better with everyday stressors. Some think self-care is about how you can feel better only immediately. Some think numbing the pain in the short-term works. However, self-care is proactive and requires you to examine the cause of your pain. It is an action that makes you feel better the next day, not wishing maybe you shouldn't have imbibed so much the night before. Self-care should not be an activity that is separate from your daily routine; it should be part of it. It means knowing what your limitations are and recognizing when you are doing more than you can handle and then trying to find out how to slow yourself down. This means getting the right amount of sleep and rest not only for your body, but also for your mind. Proper nutrition cannot be underestimated. Food is the factor on which all human life depends. Overindulging once in a while is natural, but on a regular basis can cause emotional, social, and physical consequences. By practicing your new self-dialog techniques, you will not be relying on cues from the outside, making food no longer a psychological

REWRITING YOUR LIFE STORY | 127

band aid. It is about making decisions that show you that you value yourself.

Self-care includes finding ways to decompress yourself throughout the day, not just after a long day at work. How do you decompress, rest your mind during a stressful day? Even when time is limited, you can stop what you are doing and stretch for a minute or two to refresh your mind and body. Do this throughout the day. Think of an exercise you can do to tune out the noise, like stopping what you are doing and getting a cool drink of water. Your brain needs to pause. Give some thought about stress-reducing techniques you can utilize when and where you sit or stand to do your work. Is there something you can change in the environment, maybe a flower or two? It is so important that you take the time necessary to know yourself better. Learning about yourself prepares you to know your personal limits and how to recognize your own level of sensitivity. Make a list of things you think are fun, and make a serious effort to include them in your daily grind or at least once a week. Make this plan routine, something you can look forward to each day and that does not have to be complicated. Feeding your spirit is one of the most important aspects of self-care. This may be in the form of taking a nature walk, praying, watching the sunrise or sunset, writing your gratitude list, meditating, listening to inspirational music, or audio tapes, and/or going to a twelve-step meeting. Self-care is taking the time to appreciate you.

Three major areas of self-care:

1. Care for your body.
2. Healthy diet, exercise and sleep habits.

3. Codependents will often give up sleep and other healthy physical activities in order to devote more time to the other person in a relationship.

4. These three basic routines can transform how you feel mentally and physically, but are also usually the first to be given up.

5. Care for your inner self.

6. The process of recovering from codependency.

7. Care for your community.

8. Engage in NURTURING, HEALTHY friendships and connections with your family and community.

9. The key is to be aware of codependent behaviors and stop them before they happen.

ASKING FOR HELP

A major hurdle most codependents face is acknowledging that they cannot do this alone. Because we are highly social beings, we rely on each other for learning and growth. Helping someone else does feel good and is very likely a key aspect in the evolution of our species, as hunting and gathering together was necessary for our survival. If we are hardwired to ask for help, why then is it so hard to do? First of all, we live in a world that praises self-reliance, and self-preservation. The smallest thought of asking for help can chip away at our ego and make us question our strengths and coping mechanisms. Yet, in modern times, where we are seemingly all digitally connected, the truth is that no one person can go it alone. Learning how to ask and accept help will be one of the most important skills you can use in recovery. Mind the reality distortions when it comes to asking for help. It is much easier than you may think.

Fear is the main reason so many are reluctant to ask for help. Fear of being turned down and rejected, which is personified as weak, vulnerable or a fraud leads to self-loathing. Here, fear trumps reason, and the mere risk of emotional pain activates our fight-or-flight response. Also, people can find it very difficult to articulate their needs in a way so that another can offer constructive assistance. This again is tied to your false belief system that your feelings, needs, and thoughts are outright obvious to others. No one can telepathically receive your plea for help, and therefore, you should not feel disappointed when others are not sensing your issues. Distorted thinking is usually based on irrational fears, and they cause painful and unnecessary emotional confusion. Putting unrealistic expectations on others or yourself causes undo emotional havoc. Individuals who believe that society as a whole needs to conform to their beliefs or their set of values are thinking narcissistically and being impractical. Discussing what you believe and standing up for yourself is a healthy characteristic, but, pushing your values and beliefs onto others can lead to chronic arguments and make people feel uncomfortable being around you; again, it is important to manage your expectations. Spend time journaling about your distorted thinking patterns, and you will realize you are far from the topic of everyone's lives. Anxiety is often based on an irrational fear and learning how to conquer anxiety is a challenge. Be prepared for your old thinking habits to keep tugging at you. This is dysfunctional and has probably become entrenched in you like a bad habit.

TIPS ON HOW TO ASK FOR HELP

- Be specific and concise. Clearly communicate your request in a concise manner. You need not overly explain so the party whom you are asking knows exactly what you mean and can accurately prepare for the amount of time and energy the task may take. Let them choose how much support they can lend, and, if there is something mutually beneficial; be willing to negotiate.

- You need not apologize when asking for help. As soon as you apologize, the excitement for the helping person diminishes. Needing help is nothing to be ashamed of, but apologizing casts a negative light on the action and makes it seem like you think you have done something wrong.

- Similarly, do your best not to minimize your request with phrases such as "I hate to ask…" or "Can you do me a favor". This implies that their help is menial and takes a sense of joy away from the act of helping someone or makes them feel obligated to say yes.

- Don't make it a transaction, make it personal. Emailing or texting for help is not a good idea unless you are filing a written request. Explain why the person with whom you are asking for help is uniquely skilled for the task. This tells the person they are special not just some way of achieving means.

- Don't emphasize reciprocity. While we tend to think that making the deal sweeter, by returning the favor, is a good strategy, this kind of communication makes your request seem transactional. People don't like to feel indebted to others, and a show of genuine appreciation for their aid rather than assign their efforts a monetary value is better received.

- Follow up with the person's past just expressing your thanks. People do long to feel validated and effective when they help another. Take the time to let them know what impact they have had upon your life or community.

- Practice getting ahead of the problem. If you have a situation or task that you know will be difficult for you, reach out before it becomes a full-blown challenge. This can be as easy as telling a friend that you have an upcoming family event, and asking if they can text you to check in. This approach avoids feelings of failure by having support on stand-by when the situation arises.

Exercise

Think of a problem or situation you need help with, but are struggling to ask for support for it. How would you respond to a friend who asked you for that same help? It's easy for us to be kind to others and hard on ourselves. Remind yourself that, at the end of the day, we're all just doing our best, and that can make it easier to show yourself this compassion.

WHAT IS HEALTHY GIVING?

Discussing healthy giving is very important for any codependent in recovery, especially since it is in their nature to give. The reason for giving is usually when contributing to another's well-being or personal growth. This is sometimes the trap for the codependent. Whether giving money, affection, or time...giving can be very dangerous for you, if you're a codependent. Wanting to be recognized for giving and feeling disappointed when not is the catch, as well as expecting something in return. In recovery, you will recognize that healthy giving is a choice. Give gifts of money, time, and affection because you want to from the heart, and based on a thought-out conscious decision. Secondly, healthy giving is for your own benefit and not just the recipient's. Actually, it is not even necessary for the person you are giving something to even be aware of it. There should be joy in your ability to give freely. Thirdly, you can only give what you have at the moment. That can come in the form of a prayer or good thoughts for an addicted loved one or in a smile to a grouch. Maybe it is in the form of forgiving someone for something incidentally done without any harmful meaning. There are many ways to give without giving up yourself, your power or your sense of calm. Lastly, healthy giving is done without expectation, unconditionally. There lies the blessing in giving. The motivation behind it is kindness, love and compassion, and treating those as you wish to be treated. The following are some healthy gifts for giving:

- Hugs;
- Acceptance;
- Encouragement;
- Affirmations;
- Listening;
- Compliments;

- Prayers;
- Forgiveness;
- Hospitality;
- Letters or cards;
- Time; and
- Volunteer services.

CODEPENDENCY SELF-ASSESSMENT QUESTIONNAIRE

Answer the following questions and give yourself a score of 1 for each "False" answer to odd-numbered question and each "True" answer to even-numbered questions:

1. I care more about my feelings than I do other people's feelings. **True / False**
2. I am not positive about my feelings sometimes. **True / False**
3. I am happy with my intimate relationships **True / False**
4. I look OK on the outside when I am miserable on the inside. **True / False**
5. I am OK with the type of relationships I have. **True / False**
6. I would never go on a trip/vacation alone. **True / False**
7. I am able to handle challenges directly and in a calm manner. **True / False**
8. I am not where I want to be in life. **True / False**
9. I have no problem ending an overwhelming relationship. **True / False**

10. I often say "yes" even when I mean "no". **True / False**

11. I usually feel pretty healthy. **True / False**

12. I am unsatisfied with my current relationship. **True / False**

13. I have no problem expressing my anger. **True / False**

14. I hate being alone. **True / False**

15. It is not at all difficult for me to not intervene; 'not my problem'. **True / False**

16. I wish I could change the past. **True / False**

17. My family communicated openly and effectively. **True / False**

18. I question my reasons for doing so much for other people. **True / False**

19. I take time to enjoy myself at least once a week. **True / False**

20. I find critical decision-making hard. **True / False**

Tally

Now add up your score here_____

A combined score of 20 and up indicates strong codependent characteristics as revealed in a review of the literature (Johnson, 2014; Lancer 2019; Livingston, Hall, & Ross, 2020).

7

THE ROAD TO RECOVERY

Recovery is a lifelong journey that involves the restoration of relationships with yourself, your higher power, and others. The three restorations are a part of your journey; they are interdependent. In order to grow in one type of relationship, you must also be growing in the other two. Recovery is about finding a healthy balance in all three relationships and finding productive and innovative ways to keep the balance. Some examples include finding a healthy balance between tending to others and tending to yourself, what you can and cannot change, and work-life balance. Every being is on a journey; the thing about recovery is being aware of it. Life is full of peaks and valleys. Those in recovery are OK with knowing it is dangerous but today choose to stop and smell the roses.

At the end of each day, doing 'good', and living 'good' comes down to a balancing act between emotion and reason, between your needs and the needs of others, and between problems and solutions. With recovery, there is a good chance of achieving this balance if you stay on course and do whatever is necessary to protect your recovery and stay consistent with your values. It is about being resilient, having the ability to bounce back in the face of adversity. Simply put, resiliency is the capability of coping with and rising to life's challenges you encounter during the course of your life, and coming back from them even stronger. It depends on various skills and draws from different sources of help, including meetings, counselors, sponsors, physicians, and the relationships you have with people around you.

There are four fundamental concepts to resilience:

1. *Awareness:* Acknowledging your surroundings and what is inside of your own head.
2. *Thinking:* Having the ability to rationally interpret the events going on in your life.
3. *Reaching out:* How you communicate to others to help you meet the challenges that you face, because being resilient is also about knowing when to ask for help.
4. *Fitness:* Your physical, mental, and spiritual ability to face life's challenges without becoming ill.

RECOVERY FROM CODEPENDENCY INVOLVES FOUR MAJOR STEPS:

Abstinence

The goal of recovery is to establish an internal point of control and bring your attention and priorities back to you. Having an internal locus of control means that your actions and behaviors are primarily motivated by your needs, values and feelings. This is the goal codependents are working toward in recovery. It is important for the codependent to learn how to meet their needs in a healthy way. There is no such thing as perfect abstinence because it involves people's dependency and not just putting down the drink or the drug. People need to be able to depend on one another in a reasonable manner and therefore, learn how to compromise in their relationships. In this case, recovery is about learning how to detach and not obsess about your relationship. Recovery is also about independence and self-direction rather than people-pleasing and manipulation.

Detachment

Many codependents associate detaching from another person as leaving them or no longer caring for them. True detachment isn't about cutting the other person off—it's about protecting yourself and your mental and emotional health. When you practice detachment, you stop projecting the feelings of others onto yourself and your worth. This is the process of learning to respond to people, not react to them. The difference is that reactions are instant, driven by the beliefs and biases of our unconscious minds. They are based in the moment and don't involve thinking about the repercussions of a behavior. They are survival-oriented. People in codependent relationships often respond in reactionary ways because they are so caught up in wanting to please/appease the other person. Responses are slower and more deliberate, involving the conscious mind in the decision-making process. They consider your own well-being as well as the effect on those around you. Externally, these responses may look the same, but they feel entirely different. Responses allow you to maintain control and stop yourself before continuing the subconscious behaviors you are trying to fix.

Exercise: Evaluate Your Responses

This exercise focuses on analyzing your reactions and requires you to take an honest, non-judgmental view of yourself. It is best done in writing, in a journal dedicated to recovery. The more you practice, the easier this process will become:

1. Reconsider the last situation in which you reacted negatively. For example, if someone chose not to do what you thought they should, and you got angry and felt defensive.
2. Write down the situation, how you reacted, and how you felt afterward. Then write down how you wish you had responded in the moment.
3. Take some time to think about why you reacted the way you did. What thoughts caused you to say or do that? What emotions were you experiencing?
4. Having identified the thoughts/feelings behind your reaction, look at possible beliefs that created those thoughts and feelings. Even just being aware of this makes it easier to be prepared in the future.

Awareness

Denial is one of the major patterns of codependency, as discussed in Chapter One. Codependents deny their own addiction to taking care of others and deny their own feelings and needs to stay in the cycle.

The simple fact that you're reading this book means you've already accomplished part of this step! Being able to identify that you want to change is a huge achievement. To reverse destructive habits, you need to be able to recognize what those habits are. The most damaging obstacle to self-esteem is negative self-talk and self-criticism. Starting to recognize the good things in life facilitates a big role in your happiness. Showing that you appreciate what you have will add to your overall life satisfaction. However, make sure not to confuse appreciation with gratitude. Appreciation is noting the good characteristics something, or someone has. Gratitude is a feeling of gratefulness for a person or a thing. While appreciation is a behavior and gratitude is a feeling, you can feel gratitude without showing appreciation. Gratitude becomes appreciation when you act upon it by bringing forth feelings of appreciation. For example, you may be grateful for your home, and, by taking care of it, you are showing appreciation. Appreciation is about acknowledging the value, significance and quality of things and people.

Exercise: Thought Awareness/Mindfulness

Meditation practices and guided journaling are the most effective ways to become aware of your thought patterns.

1. Find a comfortable seated position on the floor or in a chair where your spine is straight, and your shoulders and jaw are relaxed. Set a timer for five to 15 minutes (five for beginners is best).
2. Take five deep breaths to ground yourself. Try to focus on the sensations of the entire breath—the air coming in

through your nose or mouth, your chest rising and then falling as you exhale. This will help you practice awareness of the present moment (which makes it easier to respond, rather than react, to things).

3. Continue breathing naturally, focusing on the rhythm of your breath. See what thoughts come into your mind.

4. As thoughts come up, notice and acknowledge them without engaging. If you think of an upsetting situation, acknowledge the thought but don't go down the rabbit hole of negative emotions.

5. Observe your thoughts compassionately, and try to be aware of your inner dialog. What are you telling yourself in the moment? What emotions are present, and where in the body do you feel them? Approach your thoughts with curiosity. Where are they coming from? Are these thoughts really 'you', or are they part of the story you've been telling yourself?

6. If you notice you've gotten caught up following a specific thought, return your focus to your breath without shame or judgment.

Acceptance

The healing process is rooted in self-acceptance, and showing yourself compassion and understanding even in difficult times. This step is a journey all on its own, and one that can be made easier through therapy and group practices. Codependents must come to terms with the fact that they cannot solve everybody's problems. Acceptance is not the same thing as approval; you can't please everyone out of the fear they will not like you. To be real, you cannot control how other people feel about you no matter how hard you try. Acceptance doesn't happen overnight, or in a week, or sometimes even a month, it is a work in progress, and it takes effort, missteps, and baby steps. The acceptance of 'what is' defines the concept of acceptance. It doesn't mean resigning yourself to what is because that means you are taking a passive stance toward your circumstances, which is derived from hopelessness. Acceptance is a positive technique necessary to move toward taking charge of your life again. It doesn't mean your approval of the facts, just the knowledge that they exist whether you like them or not. It doesn't mean acceptance of abusive or inappropriate behavior. While this misconception is common, some are not always conscious of their abuse and do not recognize it as such. Therefore, they do not face it. With acceptance, you can make behavior changes, seeking support and safety, and begin to set boundaries.

Action

In order to grow and recover, you must combine insight with action in your day-to-day life. In some ways, this step is the most difficult, because it requires us to engage in the present moment. This means setting internal boundaries and keeping commitments to yourself. When you have no respect for yourself, it is easy to let other people create an identity for you. You have to consciously say "no" to your inner critic and the negative habits in your life. Get to know yourself. As you continue on this journey, create opportunities to reconnect with your inner self that you have repressed for so long. Intentionally explore what you like, what you value, what you want from life and relationships, etc. Practice: Set aside time each week for an activity that's just for you. In the beginning, you may try a new activity each week as you relearn what resonates with you. Recovery isn't all or nothing. Even small changes can create lasting effects in your life. Practice consistency over achievement. There is no finish line you need to rush to, just a steady pace to follow.

Exercise: Say "No" To One Request

When you state "no", you are saying it to only one option. By verbalizing "yes", you are saying no to every other choice. Codependents often find themselves committing to too many things and making time for too many people. This exercise is meant to help break the gut reaction of saying "yes" to any request.

- *First approach.* Choose a period of time that you will set aside for yourself each week. Regardless of what situations may arise, say no to anything that would eat up that time. This will not only help you practice healthy boundaries, but also create an opportunity to do some self-care.
- *Second approach.* Set a goal each week to say no to one request, and increase that number as you feel more confident in asserting yourself. When you say no, reflect on how it feels in your journal. Do you feel guilty? Think about why that might be.

Labeling

If you label your negative thinking, you can tame it. When you have an unhealthy thought that goes along with the negative emotion, mentally "label" it as a story. Then, create a self-dialog to let it go. If you repeat this process, you will be able to diffuse the story and eventually overcome the negativity. Labeling a painful process/cycle makes it easier to find solutions and steps to break those patterns. The life you live today is basically the sum of your habits. How successful, healthy, and happy you are is directly related to your habits, what you do repeatedly every day, whether it is a thought or an action, and the characteristics you portray. If you want to improve and form healthier habits, there is a helpful foundation that can make sticking to new habits easier.

Self-Forgiveness

The definition of forgiveness is usually defined as a deliberate action to let go of feelings of resentment and anger toward a person who you believed did you wrong. However, while many codependents are very good at forgiving their partners or other significant people in their lives, it is commonly much harder when it comes to forgiving themselves. It is very important to learn from your mistakes and errors, and how to let go, forgive yourself and move on. Self-forgiveness is not a sign of weakness nor is it letting yourself off the hook. It doesn't mean you condone the wrongdoing. Self-forgiveness is about acceptance of what happened and your part in what happened, and now you are ready to let it go and proceed with your life without ruminating in guilt over the past (which cannot be changed). Forgiving yourself and letting go of your acknowledged mistakes can lift you up and improve the way in which you think about yourself. One strategy for self-forgiveness implies four essential actions (the 4 Rs) that will assist you:

1. **Responsibility**: This is facing the reality of what you have done, which is the hardest part of self-forgiveness. The time for rationalizing, justifying, and making excuses for your behavior to try and make them somehow acceptable is over. It is time to 'face the music'. Acceptance and taking responsibility helps avoid excessive shame, guilt, and regret.

2. **Remorse**: You may feel guilt, shame, and other negative feelings as the result of taking responsibility. Remorse can act as an avenue to positive actions and an overall behavior change. Feeling guilty essentially means that you are a good individual who made a mistake, it is the shame that has you feeling like a 'bad' person. This gives rise to feelings of unworthiness, depression, aggression, and addiction. It is important to remind yourself that mistakes don't make a person bad nor should they undermine your personal sense of value.

3. **Restoration**: An important aspect of self-forgiveness is making amends to the person you feel you have wronged even if that person is you. Just like forgiving someone else for doing you wrong, forgiving yourself is equally important. It is likely to stay with you too, as you may feel as if you earned it. Rectifying your mistakes is one way to help you in moving past your guilt. This way, you will not have to think back and wonder if there was more you could have done.

4. **Renewal**: All people have things that they regret, but falling into self-loathing and self-pity can damage your self-worth and motivation. It is necessary to find a learning experience out of each negative situation by first

understanding why you did what you did so you can prevent the behaviors moving forward.

Recovery from codependency is not as clear as it is for the addict. The addict has a clear-cut picture of what they need to do and is not confused about whether or not they are using drugs and/or alcohol, partaking in gambling or other addictions with measurable consequences. Relapse in the form of obsessive worrying, self-pity, resentments, as well as other negative emotions can creep back into the life of the codependent before they realize it even happened, if they do not consciously work with a program of recovery on a daily basis. There may be other gray areas for the individual with codependency, such as, "Where does appropriate concern end and obsessive caretaking begin?" The challenges are considerable and cannot be handled alone. Fortunately, there is an abundance of helpful resources on the subject available to facilitate the recovery process for the codependent.

Respect and Codependency

In recovery, you will learn how to live respectfully and mindful of others. Being respectful of another person does not entail becoming a doormat. People in recovery learn to never demean themselves. Recovery is about redeeming your self-worth enough to have self-respect and respect for others. Recovery gives you the freedom to stand up for your convictions when other people treat you with disrespect. What can be more demeaning than codependency? It will drain you of your self-respect, especially if you allow someone else to treat you as less than. Through the twelve steps, you will gain the power back and learn to respect yourself. You will gain a choice in whether or not to esteem other people not just so they will approve of you or love you back, but, because respect is essential to all human interactions. There is not much mystery in recovery because it seeks only to accomplish. All beings are worthy of respect. The relationships you seek should be with others who offer mutual respect, not ones doing you a favor or wanting something in return. Everyone has to carry their own load. But, you can still and always be mindful enough to support and encourage others on your journey through recovery.

Letting go of Perfectionism

Being a perfectionist is no healthy way to live. Eventually, you will have to give the imperfect world an imperfect you. The difficulties in life are what make us grow. So, one of the best things you can do for yourself is to give up any false expectations and learn how to forgive and accept yourself as a compassionate person capable of seeing other's perspectives beyond your own. Waving a white flag to an imperfect universe will free you up to enjoy life as it simply unfolds. When you learn how to accept your own limitations, you will be free to be comfortable with yourself and give the freedom of comfortability to those around you. Leave your judgmental attitudes and idealism to the birds, and accept imperfections as a part of the beauty in life. Acceptance goes a long way toward healing any unhealthy desires you may feel compelling you to change, manipulate, fix, rescue, control, or alter another person's behavior or events in your life of which you cannot change. Clinging to past events is far too much pain for anyone. Yesterday's answers and solutions have landed you only looking for more. Practicing honesty and hard work in your life leads to better self-esteem, self-respect, and inner peace. The good news is that new answers and new solutions await you. Try to patiently encounter your future, rather than trying to control it obsessionally. To have serenity, you must fill your feelings with complete awareness while realizing you do not have to act upon them, act them out or judge them. You simply recognize your feelings and quietly accept them. Notice the circumstances producing them, and make a conscious decision on whether or not to respond.

Your personal perception of right and wrong is referred to as your moral compass. This includes your values, beliefs, traditions, and behaviors that, after much inner thinking, point the compass in either the right direction or the wrong direction. The question you need to ask yourself before you take action is, "What information do I need to make the best decision on what to do?" The answer to your question is communicated to you from your past, both good and bad memories that were similar in nature. Your understanding of how to act "healthy" and how you use the information to improve upon yourself in some way guides your behavior. These information sources together help you to decide how you can apply what you already know to any given circumstance. It is imperative that you practice self-honesty here about what you are capable of doing and what you are not, and the consequences of your behaviors in the past, so as to not repeat any previous mistakes.

Exercises: Feeling better:

- Making your bed helps you to feel accomplished and organized.

- Reading for 15 minutes during lunch is the break your brain needs from worrying.
- Daily exercise keeps you ahead of the problems life has to offer.
- Handwrite your daily goals. Follow a regular sleeping pattern even on the weekends. Re-evaluate the impossible.
- Practicing positive thinking is key to stress management. Take a block of time and use it each day to practice positive thinking. It is one of the most important aspects of recovery, happiness, and peace.

REBALANCING YOUR LIFE AND YOUR PERSPECTIVE

The focus in your life must be removed from the other person in your codependent relationship. Codependents have to make a decision wholeheartedly to switch the focus back onto themselves. The more self-educated you are, the more you will become aware of your self-defeating propensities. Giving up your codependency may at first make you feel like a monster, but as we noted before, you cannot take care of someone else while neglecting you. It can be challenging to pull back from someone you care about and to stop blaming them for your problems. People bring their family skeletons and ghosts from the past into their current relationships, and all of those traumatic and disappointing experiences affect how you interact with someone else. It is not until you can untangle the emotions connected to bad life experiences, that you can grow out of the codependent cycle. Ask yourself what role you were expected to play in your family of origin.

Examine unhealthy patterns reflected from your past into your current relationship.

Therapy and sharing at meetings are also good ways to dedicate your time to recognizing these patterns. Unloading expectations from your childhood will help you put your own needs ahead of others. Some people resist this idea because it feels like they are being selfish. Prioritizing yourself doesn't mean you have to ignore or be hurtful to others. When you are your most authentic self, the people who care about you will be even happier. Consistently denying your own needs takes you out of touch with what *you* want, and eventually leads to exhaustion and resentment. Give yourself permission to enjoy the journey. Make time for some irresponsible fun, something that will enhance your happiness, something you enjoy. Personal growth is always a process, and you may not be exactly where you want to be. Give yourself credit for how far you have come in life and appreciate the small victories.

Work toward having balanced expectations of others. Strive for healthy tolerations. You may have tolerated too much or not enough in your past or expected too much or not enough. Did you swing back and forth from taking mistreatment to refusing to even tolerate normal imperfections humans have? Even if you feel better in either extreme, it's not healthy. If you open your mind to the process of recovery, you will, at some point in time, start to transition from extremes toward balance; it is an 'aha moment'. Learning how to not confuse contentment with boredom is one of the best gifts of recovery. Breaking the chaos addiction, not having to be the VIP at your own pity party, is another gift of recovery. You are able to find your own unique journey to balance as you start and continue your recovery. Say to yourself, first thing in the morning, "Today, I will work on patience and working toward my goal of balance in my life."

People commonly sacrifice their authenticity to fit in, almost without thinking, and have been programmed in life to do so. Self-awareness sounds like a self-defining term. But it requires becoming educated to learn how to practice it. The essential aspect of being authentic is when you find what you love in life and stop basing your emotions on the expectations of others. Working too hard to try and be what others define as authentic is not how it works. Staying true to yourself or emotional self-transparency is not only about being honest to yourself, it is about the ability to receive and accept feedback, having empathy, and being humble. A chameleon protects itself by changing colors, not to protect another. Don't change yourself for another person, change for yourself. The reward is a more authentic and happier state of being, as well as improved coping skills. Make emotional self-transparency be your mission in life for staying authentic. This means having to identify all your character defects, influences, and then examining them. It is important to be able to adapt, but staying true to yourself in the process is the key to being authentic.

Balance in a Relationship

The way you know a relationship is healthy is that, when things are good, you should feel balanced and grounded. There are always going to be changes along life's journey, and sometimes they are big changes. In a relationship that is balanced, both partners give and take and change in the process together. Love does have a transforming power, so choosing a partner you can grow with is of the utmost importance. Remember, your friends and family become their friends and family and vice versa. Your partner's ability to listen, support and honor you will be the lift you need when times get tough, but if they tend to invalidate, criticize, ignore and/or abuse you, it will take you to a place that no one wants to go. This is why it is critical that you both pitch in, giving and taking the same amount of energy and support. One-sided codependent relationships, as we have fully discussed in this book, are far from healthy. A balanced relationship takes brutal honesty.

Codependents often realize but fail to mention that the power in their relationship has shifted since the seduction phase. It is not far-fetched for the codependent to adjust their schedule according to their partner's, canceling important events just to do something trivial with them. This spells bad news for the relationship. The taker in this relationship feels a need to maintain control and will eventually lose all respect for the giver, and the giver will begin to seed resentment. At that point, there is already serious trouble brewing. It isn't easy to regain equal footing just through arguing or acquiescing when you mean "no". The following are some warning signs:

1. Not visiting or accepting invitations by friends to go out, because you don't know if it is OK with your partner or you don't know their schedule yet. This also tells your partner that they do not even need to check with you prior to making any plans.
2. Do you find yourself always answering with an "I don't know" when asked to make simple choices such as what to

order on a menu in a restaurant? You might just be trying to be easy to get along with, but easygoing can sometimes mean putting someone else in control over your needs, wants, and desires.

3. Are you a person that literally follows the lead of others? Do you wait for your partner to always cross the street first or for them to turn a certain direction in the mall? Who picks the table when dining out? If you said yes to any of these, it is time to take your life back. Try taking the lead next time.

4. If your partner is only calling you when it is most convenient for them, there is a problem. Do you answer the phone or panic to answer the phone in fear you will miss a call from your partner? If you answered yes to either of these questions, your relationship is unbalanced.

5. Does your partner think it is their right to take their temper out on you? It certainly isn't anyone's right to take their frustrations out on another person. If you are uncomfortable with your partner's tone, guess what, it is a BIG deal. Tell them to stop and if they choose not to, leave the room.

The first step in creating a balanced relationship involves both people in verbalizing and listening. If the communication is not balanced, the relationship cannot be balanced. The main reason for a relationship is to create an atmosphere where both partners complement each other. It is all too common that individuals are preparing a rebuttal while their partner is talking and therefore cannot really hear a word the other is saying. People who do not know or practice skilled listening miss out on great and interesting things in life. If you genuinely listen, you will be better at problem-solving and conflict resolution. To help you to develop your listening skills, make sure to pay attention to non-verbal cues, as well as focusing on the person's words. This will aid in understanding better. Various meanings are portrayed at any given time in a discussion (were they kidding or being sarcastic?). Rephrasing a question when answering it, tells the person who asked the question that you fully understood its meaning. Take a look at your strengths and weaknesses and how they influence your decisions. To listen genuinely takes remembering what was verbalized in the conversation. Rephrasing assists your memory recall about the context of the conversation. Jumpstart your skilled listening with a bit of information gathering from various places, such as your partner's eye contact, hand gestures, facial expressions, and tone. Your partner will feel better understood if you are looking into their eyes when they speak. Take into account your partner's culture as it plays a big part in how they communicate.

Consider non-verbal gestures:

- Your hands say more than your face. Placing your hands behind your head may indicate boredom. Clasping your hands together signals dominance.
- Watch out for a blank stare and pursed lips as it may indicate anger.
- Tilting your head back when listening signals condescension (looking down your nose at someone).
- Poor eye contact and looking around when someone is talking portrays disinterest and a lack of respect (except, in

some cultures, such as the Native American Culture, where eye contact is considered a lack of respect).

- Don't think by interrupting you are showing an interest because it makes others feel misunderstood.
- Listen without judgment. Mentally criticizing impairs effective listening. It directly interferes with understanding your partner, and it takes a conscious effort and practice to get good at it.

The feeling you get when someone is giving you their undivided attention is one of ultimate respect. Poor listening skills will kill your relationship. It is the main strategy for showing you care about the person talking. Feedback validates your understanding of the conversation. The best way to show that you have listened to someone is to ask pertinent questions when they are finished talking. This tells the person they were understood. Being balanced in a relationship does not mean you always agree. In fact, you often have to come to terms with disagreeing. Balanced relationships are not conflict-free; conflict precedes all change and sometimes it is the main factor in balance restoration. The key to effective disagreeing is to mind any aggression and always maintain mutual respect. Make space for disagreeing and try to understand the other's point of view. If you are going to debate —debate with respect.

Your partner may not always, if hardly ever, do what you want. You also may not always do what they want you to do. However, having a balanced relationship requires you to consider your own wants and needs as well as your partner's. If your significant other makes decisions regularly without conferring with you, they obviously care more about having it their way than having harmony in your relationship. Unfortunately, this is all too common in codependent relationships where there is a lack of balance. Also, having balance in your life is not just about your relationship, it is about having a balance between your relationship and the other parts of your life. It is critically important to your emotional health for both people in a relationship to have independence from each other outside the relationship. If you both have a life outside of the relationship, you are able to maintain your authentic self and bring various learning experiences to your relationship. It is not always going to be perfect. There should be plenty of occasions where you need 'some space' or when you are not feeling 100% 'warm and fuzzy' about each other. That is OK. Remember, life is peaks and valleys, as are relationships.

Positivity Exercise

Sit comfortably with an aroma diffuser and list five positive thoughts to carry with you throughout your day. Share in a group meeting and with your friends that you practice every day on improving your positivity. The list of stress-related ailments is lengthy. There are thousands of books on stress management. But, the importance of self-dialog in recovery and stress management needs to be emphasized.

The Four Stages of Habit

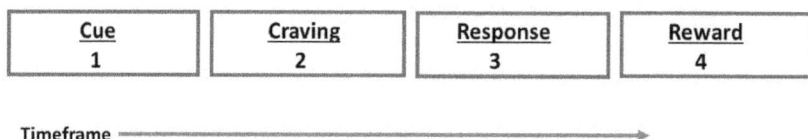

Cue	Craving	Response	Reward
1	2	3	4

Timeframe ⟶

These stages are the foundation of every habit and your brain walks through them in the same pattern each time. Firstly, the cue is what triggers your brain to begin a specific action. This small amount of information predicts a certain reward. During times of primitive man, this pattern was necessary for survival as the brain paid attention to signals that cued the places of rewards such as water, sex, and food. Today the reward cues are more in line with money, status, approval, love, praise, and power. These rewards in a way also lend themselves to survival or at least improving the quality of our lives. Your brain is constantly taking note of your internal and external atmosphere for clues as to where rewards may be. Because this clue lets us know a reward is around the corner, it naturally triggers a craving.

Cravings are the next stage in the loop of habit-forming, and they are the inspirational force backing up every habit. Without motivation (craving), we are not prompted to act. The craving is not the habit but the change in you that it creates is. It is not an alcoholic drink the addict craves; it is the feeling the drink provides. The motivation behind turning on the TV is the entertainment provided. Each craving is connected to some desire in changing your internal feelings. Cravings are unique to each individual, but the cues are pretty much the same. For the coffee drinker, the sound of the coffee maker can be a strong trigger to spark an intense craving for the beverage. They mean nothing without your interpretation. The feelings connected to the cue are responsible for the craving.

The third stage is your response. This is the specific habit you act out, which can be in thought or action. How much difficulty is associated, and your level of motivation are the defining aspects of whether or not and how you respond. If a specific behavior requires more effort either physically or mentally, then you might not respond. Habits only happen when we are able to perform them. If you want to run a mile but you have a broken leg, then, you are just out of luck. Bad habits get in the way of accomplishing your goals. They also jeopardize your mental and physical health. All of your habits—both good and bad—have a reason in your life. There is some secondary reward. Sometimes it is physical, such as the 'ahh' feeling some get from an alcoholic beverage, and some are emotional, such as the adrenaline one gets regularly when in an abusive relationship. Some habits elicit both types of response, for instance, checking your email every hour may make you feel more connected and stops you from feeling like you may miss out on something, and so you repeat the cycle. However, think of how much productivity is lost due to this habit.

Lastly, a reward is delivered to the response. Rewards are the main purpose of each and every habit. You notice the reward with a cue; then you crave the reward, then you obtain the reward. The reason for the reward is to satisfy a craving. Energy is provided by water and food; a raise produces more respect and money and working out improves your fitness and dating prospects. But the more immediate service is the satisfaction of the craving. Also, being rewarded stimulates a memory telling us how to achieve the reward again in the future. As you go about your daily routines, your brain is constantly monitoring and reminding you which behaviors deliver pleasure and satisfy cravings. Disappointing and pleasurable feelings are part of the feedback that helps you decide useful behaviors from useless behaviors. The reward completes the habit-cycle feedback loop. If the behavior lacks in any of the aforementioned four stages, a habit will not be formed. If you remove the cue, you will never start a habit. If you make an action very hard, you won't be able to do it, such as not buying ice cream to begin with. If the reward doesn't satisfy your craving, you will not have any purpose for doing it again.

How to Unlearn a Bad Habit

Unlearning a bad habit is just as important as learning a productive one. As mentioned above, a repetitive action creates a routine, which manifests as a habit over time. Getting rid of a bad habit is a learning process, and most often it is never comfortable. But that distasteful quirk can be exterminated with a bit of patience and perseverance. The codependent has bad habits, the same as the addict does. The first step in countering a bad habit is to own up to it. Taking responsibility to acknowledge that it is, in fact, a *bad* habit allows you to notice who you were before the bad habit became one, and that will give you the strength to label the toxic tendency. Coming to terms with your reality gives you a clear understanding of why change is necessary. Like with addiction, identifying your triggers is a step toward unlearning a bad habit. Take a good look at your negative tendencies, and you will come to see them as the source of your problems. If you know your triggers you will be able to act upon them when they arise. Similar to smoking, going cold turkey is challenging, but, if you substitute a positive trait for your toxic traits, you can get a hold of your undesirable ways. For the smoker wanting to quit, they will need to find other anxiety-reducing positive characteristics to replace the toxic one of smoking, such as taking a walk and taking advantage of the enormous amount of smoking cessation resources. Seeking the help of a professional isn't a bad idea if your bad habits are self-destructive.

In order to overcome a toxic habit, planning is a must. Be prepared for failure, and do not let that stifle your motivation. People often fail the first, second, and even third time they try to quit a bad habit, especially if that habit is in the form of toxic relationship addiction. Shake it off and start again. Being creative and diligent with your planning can save you from having to go back to the drawing board. Being innovative and meticulous with your planning can save you from starting all over. Learn from a failure or a stumble, it is not the end of the world (even if it feels like it) ...you're only human. Step back from your bad habit slowly and keep stepping back until it is gone. Self-dialog will take you a long way in calming the triggers. The more you tell yourself you are committed to change, the more likely your attempt to curb your toxic quirks. Again, be fearless about asking for help. Tell your support group about your goals to end a bad habit because they will undoubtedly be in your cheering section. Keeping positive people in the loop about your challenges allows them to motivate you to keep pushing.

Another way to kick your bad habit to the curb is to employ a healthy substitute. You need to plan ahead of your response stage, such as instituting a breathing exercise rather than lighting up a cigarette. Also, blot out as many triggers as you can. If you are trying to shed some pounds, don't buy ANY ice cream for example. If you are spending too much time in front of the TV, put the remote away. Simply put, make it easier on yourself to break your bad habit(s) by avoiding the triggers that ignite them. The comfortable couch in front of the TV is a perfect example of how your environment supports some bad habits and makes good ones more difficult. Change your environment, and you can change your habit. Sit at a desk when you read instead of in your bed.

Keeping track of your journey will help you to succeed in extinguishing the bad habit and replacing it with one beneficial to your happiness and serenity. Simply take to journaling your process and progress. Overcoming an unhealthy habit should be your main priority, but don't focus on the toxic behavior alone; put your energy and time into your efforts, not on targets or deadlines. Just take it a step at a time without overthinking. Stick with the winners. The codependent must work on limiting their interactions with toxic people because they serve to only amp up your toxic habit. Find creative ways to stay upbeat even in the face of adversity. You need to note your process when defeating the demons in your life, while honoring your achievements along the journey.

A good way to defeat bad habits is by surrounding yourself with people who have what you want, the way you want to live your life. See yourself as a success by visualizing yourself on top of your game, smiling in face of your success, building your new identity. Know that you do not need to be someone else's doormat, you need only become your authentic self. It is often thought that a person has to become a completely new individual in order to change their ways. But the truth is that you already have it in you to be that person without those bad habits. It is so important to monitor your self-dialog so that you do not judge yourself for not being better; remember it's baby steps. If you do employ negative self-judgment, finish the thought with the word 'but'; for instance, "I am foolish, and no one likes me, but I am working on stopping my negativity". Plan for falling off the horse every once in a while; what separates successful people from those who are not, is getting right back on the horse. Simply tracking your bad habit will help you to be more aware of the behavior and will give you many ideas for how to stop them.

Activity: Write down and answer the following:

1. When do you act out your bad habit?
2. Here's a simple way to begin: Put a piece of paper and a

pencil in your pocket and write down how many times per day/week your bad habit appears. At the end of each day/week, add them up to see your total.

3. The goal for this part of the activity is not to make you feel badly about yourself or to feel guilty for your actions. The goal here is to become more aware of the circumstances surrounding your bad-habit actions.

4. How many times per day/week do you act out your bad habit?

5. Where are you when you act out your bad habit?

6. Who are you with when you are acting out your bad habit?

7. What triggers you to act out your bad habit?

Social Support

The term "social support" often is discussed in terms of relationships. Social support means having people or a group of people to turn to when you are struggling and to help give you a wider focus and positive self-worth. Social support betters the quality of life and provides a safety net against adverse life events. For the codependent, a strong support network can be of critical importance to helping you through the difficult obstacles that arise in your recovery journey. Lacking a support network can lead to isolation, relapse, and loneliness. Social support differs from your support group, as it is with the people you turn to outside of the Twelve-Step environment. It is made up of peers, friends, colleagues, and neighbors. It needs to be cultivated, whether you are under stress or not. It will provide you with a better foundation when struggling because you know that you have a network of people there for you. A social support network does not need to be formalized. Having coffee with a neighbor, a phone call with a friend, and volunteering at a local charity are all ways to foster and develop lasting relationships with others.

The benefits of a social-support network include the following:

- Improving stress and coping mechanisms;
- Alleviating the effects of relationship distress;
- Promotes optimal mental health;
- Increases self-esteem; and
- Promotes healthy behaviors.

Having a strong social network will help to improve the quality of your life by assisting you in combating stress. Here are some helpful suggestions for creating your social-support network:

- Get involved by volunteering for a cause that is important to you. It will connect you to people who share common values and interests.
- Join the gym. Adding exercise to your daily routine will bring you a healthier lifestyle and be a great place to meet new friends who also have good health on their mind.
- Enroll in an educational activity. This will open up opportunities to meet and engage with others who share similar interests.
- Search the Internet for sites to help you stay connected with community resources and allow you to be privy to codependency literature.

All too important to note is that a social network is about the 'give' and the 'take'. Successful and meaningful relationships are a two-way street. The following are the foundation for social networks.

- Call people back who reach out to you. Return emails and stay connected.
- Identify with others, don't compete. Be happy for others' successes, not envious.
- Practice your listening skills, noting what is important to the person who is sharing their experiences or thoughts.
- Keep in mind your ability to overdo it. Do your best to keep your codependency at bay and not overwhelm your friends with controlling phone calls and/or emails.
- Take time to appreciate your social network by saying thank you and letting them know they are important to you.

The goal of establishing your social-support network is to decrease your stress level, not to add to it. Keep an eye on your energy meter so that you do not end up in a draining scenario. This means to avoid those relationships within which people are negative, critical, and needy. Steer clear of gatherings focused on drinking alcohol or doing recreational drugs. Taking the opportunity to create a social-support network is a smart investment not just for your emotional well-being but also for your physical health and longevity. When you are the one provided support or receiving support, you will reap the benefits.

Twelve-Step Support Groups

We have already touched on the background of the twelve-step support groups and how they have been proven to be effective in helping codependents. There are different types of groups; each type being designed to help a different type of unhealthy relationships. Al-Anon is a support group for those whose lives have been damaged by an alcoholic. They share experiences common amongst them and work together on creating a positive change. Alateen is for teenagers whose lives have been damaged by an alcoholic. Teenagers meet other teens with situations in common with them. Nar-Anon is a twelve-step support group for friends and families of addicts and has the same programming as Al-Anon and Alateen. All three of the abovementioned groups are essentially for those who are feeling desperately concerned about the addiction problem of someone very near to them. When entering the group, you are no longer alone but amongst real friends who understand your problem as few others could. Confidence and anonymity are always respected. Assurance is provided that there is no situation too challenging and no degree of unhappiness that is too great to overcome.

Codependents Anonymous is a twelve-step program of recovery from codependency. It is where those with codependency issues can share their experience, strength, and hope in efforts to find freedom where there has been servitude and serenity where there has been mayhem in their relationships with themselves and/or others. Many codependents have been looking endlessly for ways to solve the conflicts stemming from their childhoods, and in their relationships. Commonly, they were reared in dysfunctional families, often where there was substance abuse, some were not. In either case, individuals who seek out such support groups as CoDA have realized in their lives that they have compulsive behaviors deeply connected to their dysfunctional family systems. People who commit themselves to this simple program have usually tried to use their partners, friends, and sometimes even their children as their primary source of well-being, value, and identity to restore the emotional losses suffered in childhood. CoDA provides a method for learning how to live life rather than just survive it. CoDA members are encouraged to grow at their own pace and recover from their self-destructive lifestyles. The twelve-Step sharing technique is a way to identify compulsive control issues and find freedom from the painful aspects of their past.

Online Support Groups

There are various online locator tools to find meetings in your area or anywhere on the globe. These tools include links for AA, NA, Al-Anon, CoDA, Naranon, and many more. (See link below)

https://recovertogether.withgoogle.com/?utm_source=houseads&utm_medium=ads&utm_campaign=onlineresources&gclid=Cj0KCQiAifz-BRDjARIsAEElyGKr0VGMLxR6xM_yp2m1wIePhwrO3xbFyr8qp63PMJggIB3DbGRS81EaAt1cEALw_wcB#online-meetings

CoDA is available online at https://coda.org/find-a-meeting/online-meetings — CoDA.org.

Meetings are available in many different languages and many different topics. When you sign into your first group meeting, you will be welcomed to a safe place. Some meetings are completely virtual, while some are in person or even both.

At that first meeting is where you will learn about The Twelve Steps, The Twelve Traditions, The Promises and more. These steps, traditions, promises, and principles are the foundation of the program, in which great comfort can be found, one day at a time, as you start your journey on the path to codependency recovery. There are structure and ground rules in the meetings. There should not be any cross-talk (talking to others while someone is sharing). When you're new, you may feel the urge to question or identify with someone when they are talking. The goal is to identify and not compare, speaking only about your own experience, strength and hope. The value in these rules helps the codependent to be honest in their sharing. Some meeting formats go around the room allowing each person a chance to share. Sharing is optional. If you wonder about your personal situation, share about it first. Someone may offer something amazing to you about it.

The meetings start with introductions and readings from The Twelve Step literature resources. You may be asked to introduce yourself, and you may want to let the group know this is your first meeting. Other readings are The Twelve Steps and the Twelve Traditions. Twelve-Step programs are spiritually based, so you will commonly hear statements about a 'higher power' or God. If you are uncomfortable with this you can apply your own concept of God, such as Creator, Spiritual advisor, and the list is endless. There is no right or wrong way to work the steps, and you do them at your own pace. Spirituality allows you to strive far beyond material things. Becoming spiritually fit will help you to figure out your meaning in life, and with it, the satisfaction and happiness that come with fulfilling your purpose. Your unique spiritual guidance, from within, will help you to choose how to best act toward yourself and others. Just like a muscle in the body, spirituality can be strengthened and developed. But instead of lifting weights, you are participating in willpower, and it's better than running to the finish line; you are pursuing your purpose in life.

Meeting Makers Make It

For many codependents, recovery starts with your first attendance at a meeting. It really doesn't matter how you came to the twelve-step group; meetings will become the anchor of your recovery work. It is suggested in the beginning that you attend a meeting every day for 90 days. After which, many codependents start to ease up on their attendance and show up only during a crisis. However, staying spiritually fit is much better attained through attending meetings on a regular basis. If you only drop in during a life-or-death situation, it is very likely you will not have the same support and understanding from the group as you would if they have gotten to know you. Make a mental note that it is only one hour a day in exchange for 23 hours of happiness, joyousness, and freedom. Hope is found in meetings, and there is where you have the opportunity to spread the recovery message. At meetings is where you will likely find your sponsor.

Often the first time you hear someone at a meeting share about a topic, it is something you may have already been thinking about. You may feel amazed that another person actually does know how you feel. This is the identification component of recovery. Make sure to take names and numbers. You never know when you might urgently need someone to talk to, so you are not facing a potential relapse alone.

Aside from keeping you sane, most people feel better after attending a meeting, even when they did not consider it to be a great meeting. Investing in the meetings of the group you joined, also called your homegroup, and the fellowship is like putting yourself in the middle of the solution. Showing up regularly allows people to know you well enough to tell when you are struggling or suffering. Plus, it makes it easier to reach out for help when you are there. Your homegroup is a special place where you make a commitment to attend meetings regularly. Many people in recovery want to give back "what was so freely given to them" and stay after the meetings to clean up, such as putting away the chairs, wiping down the tables, and making coffee for the next meeting. This is referred to as service. This way, you are still making a difference in your life and the life of another codependent, no strings attached. Also, in your homegroup, you can learn how to share and get along with other codependents (i.e., learning how to agree to disagree). Members in a homegroup often feel a healthy sense of family and enjoy getting together for risk-free social events where they love and support one another.

Importance of Sponsorship

No one likes to be controlled. But you can seek guidance in the rooms of one of the twelve-step groups or with a sponsor. Sponsors are there to guide you through the steps and teach you how to live a fulfilling and happy life and can be a great inspiration for spiritual fitness. It is your choice who you pick to be your sponsor. It is smart to ensure they are aligned with your own values and goals, and that they will build you up and not bring you down in any way. Getting a sponsor is one of the most important aspects of recovery. It is how you learn to work the steps. When members of a twelve-step support group use a sponsor, the meetings tend to be very healthy as beginners already feel a sense of fellowship.

Sponsors are there for you when you need help in understanding the process or when you have a weak moment. They have the ability to be objective and dissociated from any feelings of responsibility for another's happiness and recovery. They also do not act in any abusive, controlling or critical ways that can end up with them acting like a therapist or rescuer. They are excellent examples of recovery, sources of caring support, and respectful of the member's anonymity and unique pace in recovery. The best place to start your search for a sponsor is in your homegroup. Many clubs or meeting places have lists of potential sponsors and when online you can ask the person chairing the meeting. Over a period of time, you may hear someone share something that you feel in common with and may want to check them out as a potential sponsor. Just like there is no perfect person, there is no perfect sponsor.

What to look for in a sponsor:

- They are sponsored themselves.
- Ideally, they have already worked through the twelve steps.
- Have more than a year of recovery.
- Recovery is their #1 priority.
- Have what you want in your recovery.

- Are the same gender, or otherwise not attracted to you sexually.
- Respect your right to confidentiality.
- Have the ability to listen and understand with compassion without giving advice or any rescue attempts.
- Help you to recognize codependent behaviors without shaming or blaming.
- Do not judge if you are also a member of another twelve-step program.
- Accept your individual pace.
- Communicate specifically and clearly.
- Ask questions only for a better understanding, not to manipulate or control.
- They know how to have fun in recovery.
- They have a power greater than themselves.
- Have a program in recovery that you admire.

TWELVE-STEP (FIRST STEP) EXERCISES:

Step One: "We admitted we were powerless over others, that our lives had become unmanageable" (Bill W., 1976, p. 21).

Step one is the only step you can take on your own before joining a group; which is recognizing the problem. The twelve Steps start with admitting you are powerless over others. Therefore, the end is really your beginning. Most often, codependents start the first step when they hit bottom; just like the addict. Insanity defined is doing the same cajoling over and over and expecting a different result. Accepting the truth that you are powerless over others is the end of your misery and the start of your freedom. You can dwell in self-pity until the cows come home and basically just look at the other person just standing there and watching. The only person who you can really control is the one who looks back at you in the mirror. Becoming truly emotionally independent has to come from within and from letting go of your expectations in relationships. Of course, everyone can have expectations of others that are reasonable. But, if others do not keep to their commitments or they are addicted, you are the only one who can manage the unmanageable. You can work step one and realize your life became unmanageable because you gave control over who you are to another person and now it is time to take it back.

Step One Exercises:

1. Recently, have you been attempting to influence someone or something, and even repeatedly tried with less than your desired results? Write an answer to each of the following:

- What have you been trying to influence?
- Who have you been trying to influence?
- What have been the results?

2. Who in your life or what in your life has been causing you barely tolerable stress? Who do you believe is victimizing you? Whom do you feel under the control of? Write an answer to each of the following:

- Who and what is/are causing you to feel crazy?
- Who is controlling your emotional well-being?

- What are you running from?

3. What would happen to you if you stopped trying to influence or control someone or some event? Write an answer to each of the following:

- What would you have to go through if you stopped trying to fix someone?
- What would happen to you if you stopped letting someone else control you?
- Which areas in your life reflect unmanageability?
- *Emotional health;*
- *Spiritual health;*
- *Financial well-being;*
- *Physical well-being; and*
- *Professional growth.*

CODEPENDENCY AND TREATMENT

Treatment involves individual and group therapy, education, and support where the person suffering from codependency can learn to identify behavioral patterns that are self-defeating. Sometimes, codependent individuals also suffer from drug and/or alcohol addiction, or their loved one is an addict who encourages them to use substances, too. Codependents may fall into the addiction trap due to their state of depression and stress encountered in their dysfunctional relationship. Just like getting treatment when hitting bottom with codependency, likewise the codependent should seek treatment for substance abuse.

Recovery is the joyous experience of finding unexpected meaning and value in the worrisome times and in the pain. It is about discovering what you thought to be unfathomable and sharing it with other people with whom you choose to have interactions. Recovery is about your decision to live your life to the fullest, one moment at a time. Living abundantly is what recovery is all about, but not in the pursuit of wealth; it is about the pursuit of happiness in being who you are right now and letting tomorrow come as it may. Some codependents are able to recover by joining a twelve-step program. Some codependents recognize their ailment through reading books, articles, blogs, and watching videos on the subject. Others begin recovery when their dependent partner becomes clean and sober. However, many times, codependency requires treatment on a professional level.

Psychotherapy, or talk therapy, can help individuals understand why they feel the excessive urge to fulfill everyone's needs while putting their own aside. A therapist can assist the individual in identifying codependent characteristics, and in understanding where in the first place these behaviors were adopted. Learning self-compassion is essential in healing and in changing dysfunctional patterns of behavior. In psychotherapy, an individual can learn how to acknowledge and accept repressed emotions. The therapist helps them to understand why and where codependent patterns developed in childhood and have now transferred into adulthood. Since codependents often suffer from low self-worth and tendencies toward perfectionism, learning self-care is essential to recovery. Individuals can role-play with their therapist and practice kindness in their self-dialog and forgiveness for their own mistakes. Over time, talk therapy can help lessen the codependent's urge to overcompensate. A therapist can also

facilitate individuals in improving their relationships with their partners and family members. They may educate the individual on how to
support others without enabling them. The therapist in
psychotherapy may also help the person to improve their ability to be
assertive.

Group therapy is one treatment protocol shown to be an effective
treatment technique for codependency. The dynamic of the group
gives the codependent a chance to form healthier bonds with others
in a safe and appropriate environment. Improved communication is
often a key goal of family therapy. Issues that have never before been
talked about in the family may be discussed in therapy. Sometimes,
one person changes (such as getting sober or encouraging someone to
be more independent), and it has a ripple effect on the entire family
dynamic. Group therapy allows the special opportunity to provide an
individual with validation from other members who have similar
treatment goals and who are experiencing similar difficulties. These
sessions are led by one or more facilitators who are specially trained
for implementing proven techniques for managing challenges specific
to codependency. In the beginning, the thought of participating in
group therapy can seem daunting. After all, who wants to 'air their
secrets' with strangers or people they hardly know.

Group therapy allows the members to provide support to one
another. Listening to others with common issues can help you realize
that you're not alone in having struggles, whether you're grappling
with an addict, an abusive partner, low self-esteem, or another codependency issue. Many people who have participated in a group-
therapy setting experience a sense of relief. When discussing prob-

lems with others, the group functions as a sounding board and can help you view things currently happening in your life that you don't see. You get a broader range of perspectives on your circumstances that can help you cope better with your problems. A group approach to therapy can propel the member forward through encouragement. Listening to others discuss how they overcame their dysfunctional helping can be an inspiration for others to push themselves harder toward recovery. Group therapy not only eases feelings of isolation, but also facilitates the member to practice healthy communication with people, so that the member can see that it is possible to get along with others. It is also less expensive than one-on-one therapy sessions. Groups provide a metaphorical mirror, and the member gets to see themselves through the eyes of another.

Some group therapy approaches utilize *cognitive behavioral therapy* (CBT), which facilitates the new learning of specific skill-building strategies. Other group therapy approaches institute the twelve-step model, previously discussed, with the goal of acceptance, increasing self-esteem and the verbalization of feelings. CBT helps the codependent change negative and dysfunctional patterns in their thought processes and belief system necessary for changing their behavior. The CBT treatment approach aims to educate the codependent individual on how to acknowledge their own problems as separate from other people's problems. CBT is a type of talk therapy that is used to treat individuals who need help with their thinking patterns, emotions and behaviors. While many think of individual therapy as exploring repressed memories from childhood, CBT focuses on exploring solutions for today instead of continuous processing of the root cause of where the codependent traits are coming from. The CBT approach is designed in a structured manner with a limited number of sessions. Identifying negative or distorted thinking patterns, so the person can see difficult situations more clearly and learn how to effectively respond to them, is one of the essential components of CBT. It aids the codependent in recognizing how their thinking patterns are affecting their actions. While the way you're thinking and responding may be based on past experiences, CBT doesn't focus on your past, it focuses on finding a solution now.

In a CBT setting when first meeting with a therapist, the codependent person will likely spend time filling out assessments so the therapist can get to know their circumstances. The therapist may also inquire about their physical, mental and spiritual health, and if they have any coexisting mental health issues, such as depression, anxiety, addiction, PTSD, bipolar disorder, borderline personality disorder (BPD) or any other conditions that may affect their feelings and behaviors. The reason for these assessments is to aid the therapist in formulating a specific treatment plan tailored to the person's specific needs. It may take more than one session. The more honest and open codependent is from the beginning, the less difficult it will be for the therapist to gather enough information to start moving them forward in their treatment goals.

Like most therapeutic processes, CBT can be challenging and emotional to go through. Learning how to change your thinking patterns about circumstances in life that have been very painful can be difficult. But, if you stay the course with your treatment plan, you can find the relief you never thought possible and experience life-changing and long-lasting changes. Here are some important things to bear in mind with CBT:

- *Honesty is a must.* If you are unable to be honest with your counselor, CBT will not work for you. It is not the type of therapy where the facilitator has to explore your thinking patterns over the course of many weeks or months trying to get an accurate picture of your life. This can prove to be very challenging for a person who is used to guarding their thoughts due to fear of rejection or a loss of control. But, the therapist is highly trained for assisting you with processing negative thinking and replacing it with beneficial and appropriate thoughts.
- *Follow through with the work provided.* If journaling is suggested by your therapist, then by all means, journal. It is in your best interest to complete your assignments so that you can enjoy the fruits of your labor.
- *Ask questions.* If you are involved in the participation of CBT the entire time, you will reap the most benefits. It is OK to question the process because your therapist is not going to shame, intimate, blame, or ignore you. Also, by asking questions, your treatment plan can be continuously revised to meet your needs.

Family therapy examines the dynamics of the dysfunctional family. Each member of the family learns how to acknowledge their patterns of dysfunction and works on improving their relationships. The goal of family therapy is to improve communication between members and to bring up difficult issues that have never been appropriately addressed. When and if one member of the family changes their behavior, it affects the whole system. Family therapy's goal is to lower the stress and provide conflict resolution by improving the interactions between members of the family. Family therapy doesn't necessarily mean only blood relatives, it can mean any system within which family-type dynamics occur. Rather than primarily focusing on the individual's role in the problem, family therapy identifies systems and patterns in the problems that need adjusting. Family therapy can be helpful for all involved on many different levels. Family therapy sessions facilitate the following:

- The development and skills to maintain healthy boundaries.
- Communication and family cohesion.
- Improve problem-solving skills by having a better understanding of the dynamics in the family.
- The ability to understand and build empathy.
- Conflict resolution with the family.

Some techniques use a *multi-family* therapeutic approach where an intensive focus is on the specific dynamics at work within a family. This strategy widens the perspectives of the family members and aids in the understanding of the treatment process. It also creates an empathetic and understanding community environment in which the family members can interact, provide constructive feedback, and process their experiences in a safe place with families who share similar concerns. The families essentially learn from each other. Being involved with a family member's treatment can very often feel like an isolative experience. It is common for the codependent's family members to feel overwhelmed, angry and scared. Though every individual's and their family's journey through treatment is unique, many of the experiences can overlap. This is why multi-family therapy sessions can help members know they are not alone. At first, the members of the family may feel uncomfortable and anxious sharing their difficulties, the codependent in treatment has already become family with group processing and may often take the lead in sharing first in the multi-family group setting. There is something very powerful in family members hearing similar experiences of other families struggling through the codependent-treatment process. Listening to one another in this type of group setting helps families learn about particular challenges other families are suffering, and can therefore, better accept the process. Multi-family sessions can assist in the development of understanding and compassion, by listening to other individuals who are struggling with codependency. When families have a chance to be a part of a greater group of individuals facing similar circumstances, challenges, and making similar efforts to change and grow, there is a propensity to leave feeling inspired and encouraged to continue.

SELF-EVALUATION

It is up to you to identify your needs, and then figure out a healthy way to have them met. It is far from reasonable to think that any single person is capable or wants to meet your every request. You are responsible for asking for what you need, as well as whether or not to respond to other people's requests. If you try to manipulate another person to be there for you, that is codependency rearing its ugly head. There is a big difference between asking and demanding something from a person. If someone is unwilling to be there, you need to change your expectations; do it for yourself. It is important to begin to let go of feeling that you have to rush through life, letting go of the constant urgency to win the rat race. A major problem about being part of the rat race is that you lose yourself because you're trying to become like everyone else. If you have to get up each morning and act out someone else's life, you are no longer in touch with yourself, and it feels awful. Living in 'your own skin', the way you choose to live, you will understand the meaning of self-pride. Getting out of the rat race means being unapologetically yourself and sharing your story, both the good and the bad. This way, you can connect to people on a different level by being yourself and not anxious about sharing your wrongdoings as well as the things you have done well. Only talking about your success stories is on the surface level. Going deeper and talking about the mistakes you have made, the tough times, and misjudgments is a cleansing process.

'Attitude' is a frequently overlooked secret of serenity. By choosing to maintain a healthy and positive attitude about everything in life, in the past, and in relationships, you can essentially control the quality of your recovery on a moment-by-moment basis. Of course, you cannot always control the situations life throws at you, but you can control your attitude about them. If you don't, life can become invariably out of control and messy. It is merely a matter of making a choice on how you will react to situations presented in life. Sometimes, a particular circumstance will come your way that is so toxic or painful that you will have to permanently leave the situation just to stay sane. If the source of the problem is too much to bear, you can leave, guilt-free, so you are practicing self-preservation. If you think you can realistically improve your situation to be healthier, that's fine, but if you keep trying to fix something that cannot or will not be fixed, in spite of your best attempt, that is when it becomes insanity. If you spend your time in negativity, thinking only about the future and the past, there is no room for the present. Think about what exists right now because it is the only reality. The past is gone, and no one knows what lies ahead. Your brain is so powerful that it has you sensing physical pain from a memory of your past. It is completely understandable for individuals to spend some amount of time thinking about the past and projecting about the future. Past experiences, whether good or bad, are a necessary survival tool. Without them, we cannot learn from our mistakes.

In order to soften your attitude toward yourself, it is important to go after the things you enjoy. By doing things you genuinely enjoy, you allow yourself the chance to experience your own pleasures and other people in an unconditional way. Create a baseline for your self-worth that you consciously cannot descend below. Feeling a sense of worth does not mean you are ego-centric or full of yourself. An ego-centric believes they are the best at everything whether it is true or not. Valuing yourself means you are going to try and do your best, but a single action does not define you. Try and be a role model to yourself with a new way of behaving. This will ease feelings of not being good enough for yourself and for those around you. We are a success-oriented society, but we are not a commodity, and we need a society that can tell the difference between the two and assists us in seeing that one person does not define another. By appreciating yourself and practicing self-care, you can create a positive change that has an outward ripple effect.

Everyone compares themselves to other people, and you can be sure that those who you think have everything surely do not. If you look at other people through the eyes of understanding and compassion rather than judgment and jealousy, you are better equipped to see them for who and what they are—humans, just like you. Always know there is more right with you than can ever be wrong with you. Many codependents zero in on their perceived flaws. It is helpful to note the positives about yourself and love the fact you are alive and able to take whichever paths you choose in life. Before you can achieve anything in the present, you must first rid yourself of the shame and guilt you feel about your past. Even if it is small, have something to look forward to. Similar to caring for yourself, having something to look forward to can be very rewarding. There is a ridiculous amount of pressure in this world to perform, which is very difficult in challenging times. But the mind and the body do find enjoyment in small things, such as your morning cup of coffee, taking the scenic route, and sleeping in. Tell yourself it's OK to enjoy the moment. The meaning you assign to events in your life impacts you more than you know. When it seems like all is doomed, your outlook decides your response. Make room for your new behaviors, if your old ones are no longer serving you. Try your best not to hold on to bad habits. When it seems like your life is falling apart, it is actually laying the groundwork for its reconstruction.

Take a page from Al-Anon's Twelve Steps and practice progress and not perfection. Striving for perfection leads only to feelings of worthlessness and self-pity. Realize that just by putting yourself on the right path is an accomplishment in itself. Instead of putting yourself down and falling down, pat yourself on the back for coming as far as you have and continuing to make progress. Telling yourself that you will only fail will not make you more successful. If you say to yourself that you are not living up to your full potential, it will not help you climb the ladder. Telling yourself you are not enough will not make you enough. It may sound almost easy, but the only road to achieving love for yourself is to love yourself, regardless of where you have been, where you stand, and even when you know you want to change. You are enough, and every time you tell that to yourself, loving yourself will become easier.

FINAL THOUGHTS

Codependency, if left untreated, gets worse. It can lead to severe depression, anxiety and potentially even suicidal tendencies. However, codependency is a condition that can be successfully treated with individual, group, and family therapy and by participation in twelve-step meetings. Usually, treatment protocols rely on a variety of therapy techniques. Client-centered therapy, as well as CBT, can be effective in treating codependency. Twelve-Step programs, such as Al-Anon Nar-Anon, and Codependents Anonymous, are beneficial to the successful treatment of codependency. Trauma therapy may also be advised for individuals who have experienced abandonment or abuse. If you have lost sight of your authentic self and question whether or not your relationships are healthy, remember there is help out there for you. If you are suffering from your own form of clinginess and feel trapped in a one-sided relationship, chances are you are codependent. Even though you're motivated by wishing the best for your loved ones, your do-good habits have become toxic to all involved. After reading this book, it is sincerely hoped that you know you have people and places to turn to in your darkest hours. When you learn to deeply value yourself and become less reactive to other people's opinions and do not take rejection personally, you become willing to lose another rather than lose yourself. The tools supplied in this reading will help you to turn self-loathing into self-love and to begin to take back control over your life and your decisions, to return to your authentic self. In fact, you've already taken the first step in gathering the information provided here to start your recovery journey.

When an individual is caught in the trap of codependency, they believe their own needs are not important. Even though the codependent often looks like the 'healthier' of the two partners, they struggle with their issues that cause them to believe they are less important than the other. Their insatiable need for approval trumps all other needs. By continuously diminishing their own wants, needs, and feelings, and looking to someone else for validation, the result is an unhealthy relationship for both. All in all, being codependent is not good for anyone involved, despite the false acts of gratitude they may receive for being so skilled in giving. Recovery from codependency takes deep self-examination and thinking things through, rather than simply acting upon an impulse to rescue. Recovery is about no longer taking everything in life so seriously; it is about learning how to love, live, laugh, and about having fun on your journey. You can find something that you enjoy doing, that is healthy, and do it for the sheer pleasure you receive.

There will always be times when giving feels like the right thing to do, and yet, there are times when that very same action is codependent. In order to distinguish between the two, an individual must be able to delve into their inner wisdom. If unable to reach inside for solutions, asking for help is imperative. Twelve-step meetings, therapy, sponsorship and researching the Internet are all excellent ways to approach the matter. Taking the time to think about your feelings and needs, and how to best address them each day, is a helpful tip for the codependent. Always remind yourself that you have a choice and the power to say "No", even when it is very hard to do so. Practice pausing before answering "yes" to anything asked of you. There is nothing wrong with saying, "I have to think it over and get back to you". Then, examine the action you may take in the situation if you were not afraid or felt obligated. Use spiritual exercises, such as journaling, nature walks, meditation and quiet contemplation to tap into your inner wisdom. Do your best to tolerate another person having a bad day or unhappy feelings without you being there to fix them.

Those who suffer from codependency can receive the help they need from many of the aforementioned resources. Twelve-step programs, such as Al-Anon, CoDA, Nar-Anon, and other non-professional fellowships, offer no precise diagnostic criteria or definition for codependency. They do freely share from their own experiences the characteristic traits and behaviors that describe their own histories of the struggles they face and have faced with codependency. Twelve-step recovery begins with self-honesty about their inability to maintain healthy relationships with themselves and with others. Finding the cause for much of their grief lies in longstanding destructive behavior patterns.

Being codependent is an emotional and a mental problem that affects the interactions and connections made with others in an interpersonal relationship. It creates major difficulties and creates great discomfort with themselves, resulting in unfulfilling and often abusive circumstances. Hopefully, by reading this book, you will be more likely to verbalize your true feelings and not be afraid that it will upset someone or hurt them in any way. Otherwise, you end up bottling up your feelings, and then they come out in the form of an illness or rage. By reading this book, you have learned:

- What codependency is and isn't.
- The history of codependency and how it has evolved over time.
- What a healthy, balanced relationship looks like compared to a toxic, codependent one.
- To understand why you act the way you do, and the possible causes of codependent tendencies.
- How to recover from being codependent and focus on your own life again.
- Different options for recovery and how to use counseling, treatment and group settings most effectively in your life.
- How to self-assess your behavior in relationships and reflect on what caused you to become this way.
- The steps to recovering from being codependent.
- How to say "No" and set boundaries with the people in your life without feeling guilty.
- The importance of getting a sponsor or professional therapist.

SOURCES

American Psychiatric Association. Diagnostic and Statistical Manual of Mental Health Disorders. American Psychiatric Association. 2013.

Bacon, I., McKay, E., Reynolds, F. et al. The Lived Experience of Codependency: An Interpretative Phenomenological Analysis. Int J Ment Health Addiction 18, 754–771 (2020). https://doi.org/10.1007/s11469-018-9983-8

Bandura, A. "Social Learning Theory". Englewood Cliffs, NJ: Prentice Hall. 1977

Barnett, J.E., Baker, E.K., Elman, N.S., & Schoener, G.R. "In pursuit of wellness: The self-care imperative". Professional Psychology-Research and Practice, 38(6), 603-612, 2007.

Beattie, Melody. "Codependent No More: How to Stop Controlling Others and Start Caring for Yourself". (Center City, MN): Hazelden, 1992.

Belyea, D. "The Effect Of An Educational Intervention on the Level Of Codependency Among Graduate Counseling Students". Wayne State University Dissertations. 2011. https://digitalcommons.wayne.edu/cgi/viewcontent.cgi?article=1208&context=oa_dissertations

Cherry, K. "Taking the Steps to Forgive Yourself". Very well mind, 2020. https://www.verywellmind.com/how-to-forgive-yourself-4583819

Codependents Anonymous Inc. "Recovery from Codependence". Codependents Anonymous Inc. 2013. www.coda.org

Cleveland Clinic. "Dependent Personality Disorder". Cleveland Clinic. 2014. http://my.clevelandclinic.org/neurological_institute/center-for-behavorial-health/diseaseconditions/hic-dependent-personality-disorder.aspx

Field, M. "My Day Depends on Me: How to rewrite your life narrative". Balboa Press, 2019.

Friel, J.C. "Codependency assessment inventory: A preliminary research tool". Focus on the Family and Chemical Dependency, 8(1), 20-21. 1985. https://doi.org/10.1016/S0899-3289(10)80005-7

Johnson, R.S. "Codependency and Codependent Relationships". BPDFamily.com. (2014).

Hinkin, C. & Kahn, M. "Psychological Symptomatology in Spouses and Adult Children of Alcoholics: an examination of the hypothesized personality characteristics of codependency". Int J Addict. 1995 May; 30(7):843-61. doi: 10.3109/10826089509067010. PMID: 7558473.

Lancer, D. "Shame: The Core of Addiction and Codependency" Psychology Today, 2019. https://psychcentral.com/lib/shame-the-core-of-addiction-and-codependency/

LePera, N. "How to Tell the Difference Between Empathy & Codependency" mbgMindfullness (2019). https://www.mindbodygreen.com/articles/difference-between-empathy-and-codependent-behavior-for-hsps

Lindley, N. R., Giordano, P.J., Hammer, E. D. Codependency: Predictors and psychometric issues. Journal of Clinical Psychology, 55, 59-64. 1999. https://doi.org/10.1002/(SICI)1097-4679(199901)55:1<59::AID-JCLP5>3.0.CO;2-M

Livingston, A., Hall, C. & Ross, G. "An Exploratory Assessment of Codependency in Student-Athletes". Athens Journal of Sports - Volume 3, Issue 3– Pages. 2020 207-224https://doi.org/10.30958/ajspo.3-3-4.

Loverde, M. "What Is Codependent Personality Disorder?" Family Intervention (2019). https://family-intervention.com/blog/what-is-codependent-personality-disorder/

Prest, L.A., Benson, M.J., Protinsky, H.O. "Family of Origin and Current Relationship Influences on Codependency". Family process. (1998) [Pubmed]DOI: 10.1111/j.1545-5300.1998.00513.x

Jenner, N. " Controlling Codependency: Keeping Others In Line". Dr. Nicholas Jenner (2019). https://theonlinetherapist.blog/controlling-codependency-keeping-others-in-line/

Rosenberg, R. "The Human Magnet Syndrome: Why we love people who hurt us." Morgan James Publishing (2013).

Staff, H. (2008, December 7). Letting Go of Perfectionism, Healthy-Place. Retrieved on 2020, December 19 from https://www.healthyplace.com/relationships/serendipity/letting-go-of-perfectionism

Sarkar, S., Mattoo, S. K., Basu, D., & Gupta, J. "Codependence in spouses of alcohol and opioid dependent men". International Journal of Culture and Mental Health, 8(1), 13–21, 2015. https://www.tandfonline.com/doi/abs/10.1080/17542863.2013.868502

W., Bill. Alcoholics Anonymous: The Story of How Many Thousands of Men and Women Have Recovered from Alcoholism. New York: Alcoholics Anonymous World Services, 1976.

SUGGESTED RECOMMENDATIONS

Please note: Your tallied results from this questionnaire cannot be considered as any type of diagnosis and, therefore, should not be understood as such. They merely indicate the potential need to investigate codependency further. The tallying system was based on a review of the literature, and points were assigned to symptomology most often reported as problematic signs of codependency.

Score: Below 6

If your score was below 6, you most likely know how to set your boundaries and may just be very sensitive and empathetic of others.

Score: Between 6 and 11

You may be ruminating about other peoples' opinions of you. Boundaries are sometimes difficult to establish. Your self-worth is not where it should be. You see yourself as a rescuer as a positive characteristic, even when it is not.

Score: Between 11 and 20

Your self-esteem is low. Codependency is flaunting itself in many areas of your life. You most likely are struggling with anxiety and approval seeking. With this score, it is recommended that you gather more information regarding codependency, including attending an Al-Anon or CoDA meeting and/or talking to a professional.

Score: Between 11 and 18

If you scored between 11 and 18, you definitely face challenges with feeling invisible, low self-esteem, and are with codependency issues most likely in many areas of your life. You may suffer from anxiety, rumination, and an ongoing need to gain approval from outside of yourself. In spite of being overly empathetic to the needs of other people, there is a good possibility you feel continually let down by others in your life. You may be someone who absolutely believes is doing everything right, but yet, no matter how hard you try, you never feel good enough for yourself or for others. Shame, guilt and self-doubt may be a constant in your life. You are someone who will benefit greatly from learning about how to heal from the patterns that were created when you were a young, powerless child.

Milton Keynes UK
Ingram Content Group UK Ltd.
UKHW042156050124
435571UK00003B/65